MANAGING
EXPECTATIONS

MANAGING EXPECTATIONS

A MEMOIR IN ESSAYS

MINNIE DRIVER

HarperOne
An Imprint of HarperCollins*Publishers*

MANAGING EXPECTATIONS. Copyright © 2022 by Minnie Driver. All rights reserved. Printed in the United States of America. No part of this book may be used or reproduced in any manner whatsoever without written permission except in the case of brief quotations embodied in critical articles and reviews. For information, address HarperCollins Publishers, 195 Broadway, New York, NY 10007.

HarperCollins books may be purchased for educational, business, or sales promotional use. For information, please email the Special Markets Department at SPsales@harpercollins.com.

FIRST EDITION

Designed by Yvonne Chan

Library of Congress Cataloging-in-Publication Data is available upon request.

ISBN 978-0-06-311530-9

22 23 24 25 26   LSC   10 9 8 7 6 5 4 3 2 1

For my mother, Gaynor

And for my English teachers,
Alastair Langlands, Graham Banks, and John Batstone

Perhaps that's what I feel,
an outside and an inside and me in the middle.

—SAMUEL BECKETT

CONTENTS

SURPRISE

I am nine and being returned to boarding school. It is Sunday night, and the clocks haven't gone back yet so there is still light as we pull up to a traffic light, next to a dark blue Volvo. I roll down my window.

"HELP ME!" I scream. "I AM BEING ABDUCTED!" The driver of the Volvo looks embarrassed, which is the chosen response to most public displays if you're British. My mother leans forward and gives him a wave and a thumbs up, the light turns green, and I see his relief as driving etiquette mercifully prevents him from further investigation. As we pull away, I leave him with a howling "CALL THE POLIIIIIIICE!" and proceed to start taking off all my clothes and throwing them out the window. My rage and sadness are not an act. I am dumbstruck with horror at the thought of going back to boarding school, and each time I am returned at the end of a weekend away, I try to explain this to my mother. My protestations have now reached operatic levels of desperation, as she is resolute in ignoring my desire to stay at home and be a day student. We live three miles from the school—it makes no sense. But it makes sense to my mother.

In the UK, in 1976, women were finally allowed to apply for a mortgage without a male co-signer. In that same year, my mother decided to leave my father and got to experience what an anomaly of social progression the mortgage thing actually was. As my parents weren't married, the judge in the family court decreed that for my mother to retain custody of me and my sister, Kate, she had to: (1) be married; (2) have bought a house; and (3) have us in school by the time she had relocated. The amount of time the judge gave her to accomplish all these things was seven weeks.

What impossible *nonsense* has been thrown at women down through the ages, and how tirelessly do they continue to rise to the challenge. My mother would not be outdone by some bewigged distillation of the Victorian patriarchy and proceeded thus: she sold everything she owned, including a small number of shares in my dad's company, and bought a dilapidated small cottage in the middle of Hampshire in England. She then cheerfully told the man she had begun a relationship with that they were getting married, and after that, marched into the school where she herself had gone and said they had to take her children (school fees pending in the nearish future) in the name of EQUALITY. My mother was always very sure of her plan. When things didn't work out, she dwelt on the failure for about a heartbeat and in the next breath had a fully formulated new plan and her own 100 percent commitment to it as backup. She had longed for and waited for my father to leave his wife. Religion, respect, and wanting to have his cake and eat it too meant that he hadn't, in all the time they had been together. He loved my mother with all his heart but felt safer keeping her as an eternal exit from the marriage and devotion he felt to his wife and the daughter they had together. After sixteen years, the exit exited.

We arrive at a falling-down cottage called Mildmay (very swiftly renamed Mildew); it is late August and I am six. Mum wears an Hermès scarf around her head, an impeccable cashmere sweater, and the dirtiest jeans, covered in mud, with Wellington boots to match. She is the sartorial embodiment of her own dichotomy: one half chic, model, designer, and wit; the other, hands deep in the earth, growing her own vegetables, and never giving a second thought to the planes over New York or the boats in the South of France that she could be sitting on.

"SO, what do you think?" She stands, smiling, holding a bagful of our things from home. She has just told us that we are moving here, to this place, that Dad will not be coming with us, and that it is going to be a great adventure.

"It's shit," I mutter.

"What did you say, Minnie?"

"I said, 'it's SHIT.'"

Then I run away. I run to the back of the cottage we have just arrived at and throw myself into the tangled jungle that is back there. We've been staying all summer with some friends in another part of the countryside, and I had been told that morning that we were going for a drive and that there was a surprise where we were going. "Surprises" are very well branded as a good thing, when everyone knows in their soul that surprise is actually a form of aggression. To that, I respond in kind.

I fight my way through the high grass and discover a chicken-wired fruit cage full of wildly growing raspberries, blackberries, red currants, and black currants. *Even the fruit is in prison*, I think. At the end of the garden, I find an old fence and a paddock beyond with a fat horse in it. I click my teeth at him, and he comes trotting over and lets me pet his nose till he realizes I don't have any food, then he tosses his head back and stands looking at me with slight betrayal.

"Oh, horse." I say. I then lay my chin down on the fence and cannot believe this is what's happening. Is this how it goes? You think you live in one place and the next you don't, it's just gone, and you find yourself thrown into a story you are expected to inhabit. Where are the people whose story this place had been, now? Are they in my old house, looking up from my bed at the light with the unicorn on it? Are they staring in disbelief at our lovely new sofa? I look back at the cottage, dark streaks of damp mottle its back wall; it is a place I feel we've visited before and couldn't wait to get away from.

I drag my feet, walking back to the front of the cottage. Little, patent town shoes squish through the mud, already scuffed from their country interaction. Longing for pavement, I arrive at the front door. Our mother's chief concern about us living in London has been the disconnection from nature. Often, when driving along a highway, she would pull the car onto the hard shoulder, turn on the hazard lights, and force march us up an embankment, and over the roar of traffic, shout the names of roadside flora.

"CAMPION. CELANDINE. ELDERFLOWER."

I do not know if what nature can give me will make up for what has seemingly been taken away, my dad foremost among those things.

A brown Ford Escort is parked outside the gate to the cottage and a man is walking up the path toward me. Mum comes flying out the door and hugs this man.

"Min, say hello." I look at him, at the hugging, and surmise that he is why we have left London, our home, our new sofa, and Dad. The man smiles distantly at me, and I say to him,

"You are why there is all this . . . trouble." I reach for the word because there doesn't seem to be one big enough to encompass what on earth is going on. He smiles more, thinking I am joking. I go on.

"You. Did. This."

"Minnie, that's enough," Mum says sharply.

Perhaps we'd all have thrown in the towel right then on the doorstep if any of us had known that it was just the beginning. For the next two years, a simmering tension runs as background noise to the honeymoon period of my mother's new marriage. My sister and I go as day students to the boarding school Mum has insisted accept us, but each evening, crammed around the tiniest kitchen table, our knees knocking against each other in horrible familiarity, I glare at this step-person. My mother's plan has, against all odds set by the British legal system, worked out. She has not made allowance, however, for its component parts to not get along quite so viscerally. My stepfather and I are definitely at odds.

I take up a lot of space, my sister is much quieter than I am, but together we are an unavoidable reminder to my mother's new husband, of her previous life, and we are definitely a bulwark between him and her sole attention. I don't know what he had thought it would be like being married to a woman with two small children. This, combined with the fact that Mum has never really taken care of us by herself—without the help of a nanny—makes me think that their plan (however satisfying sticking it to the courts might have been) was not something they have actually thought through.

I am the helpful herald, pointing out the cracks, sometimes using anger to alert them to the particularly big problems in this new dynamic.

The cottage is so small, it is impossible to pick sides and create enough space to feel the power of your particular faction. We are all constantly on top of each other, having to navigate the necessity of turning our backs to the wall to face each other as we shuffle past in the hallway. Mum has become this co-opted stranger; I want to rescue her and remind her that we are love and he is an interloper. But she has chosen him to forge a new life with, and for all his vague annoyance at our presence, his shouting and inability to find common ground with us, Mum's need for this marriage to work supersedes everything for a lot of reasons.

The place my stepfather and I clash the most is around mathematics. He sits in a room with me and tells me to learn my times tables. I look at the numbers for a while, I appreciate their patterns, but their representations are too vast for me to comprehend, too mysterious, and instead of wanting them to reveal their secrets, I prefer their mystery. I have no intention of turning my brain into scrambled eggs making sense of something whose impenetrability I actually find beautiful.

"If you don't learn to do math—to multiply and add in your head—you will not be able to function in the world."

"I shall have a calculator."

"You won't always have a calculator."

"Yes, I will."

"You shouldn't need a calculator; you have a perfectly good brain."

"Why? Why shouldn't I? Calculators do math, my brain does other things."

"Math teaches you logic."

"I don't get math! It is *logical* for me to have a calculator."

At this point, red in the face at my obstinance, he tells me to stay in the room until I have written out all the multiplication tables. As soon as he is gone, I run for the door, take the stairs two at a time, and lock myself in the cottage's only bathroom. Soon, there is pounding on the door and some threats, then the loud assertion that he is going to get a drill and take the door off its hinges. There is a tiny window in the bathroom that opens upward like a hatch. I am small enough to crawl through and then able to stand on a small amount of flat roof outside. It's too far to jump down, but our neighbor's oak tree leans helpfully across the alleyway at the side of the cottage, and I can jump for its nearest branch quite easily, and with a fireman's pole slide, be on the ground in seconds.

I have learned fast that running away is an adrenal choice, and your escape is determined by how calm you can remain while your little synapses are firing madly and your body floods with super small-girl strength. I also realize that nine out of ten plans fail when you don't know where you're going. I always head to the woods, and the only hazard between my getting there or not is the neighbor into whose garden I now jump.

I only know him as Gavin Gipson's dad. Mrs. Gipson and her kids, Gavin and Lorna, have moved out. Gavin's dad doesn't make a lot of noise; his silence is strange and has a low hum of menace about it. What is even stranger is the fact that he never wears pants. I don't just mean trousers; I mean pants in the British sense of "underwear." He wears T-shirts and wellies in the garden, clipping back his roses, backside to the sun and the windows of our galley kitchen. Once, when I had knocked on his front door, collecting signatures for a petition on behalf of Greenpeace, he had answered the door in a shirt and tie and suit jacket, penis just visible beneath the hem of the shirt. I knew everything about this was wrong and determinedly looked him in the eyes and carried on telling him about the plight of the whales. Grown-ups are an absolute mystery, and I'd found if I just took them at face value and didn't get involved in their motivations, their personal shit would always be recognizable as something that belonged to them and had nothing to do with me. This is how I give context to Gavin's dad's penis, but I also really want to avoid it at all costs.

I duck down behind the hedge that divides our two front gardens and scuttle to the gate and out onto the road. Kate is leaning against a low wall, someways up the street, apparently waiting for me.

Referring to our stepfather, I ask,

"How did you know I'd be here but he doesn't?"

"He's too busy finding the right drill bit for the screws on the bathroom door hinges. Apparently they are tiny and Victorian."

"I'd better not hang around. Do you want to come up to the woods?"

"Yeah, Barrow's sweet van just pulled up, up the road. Let's go there first."

"I don't have any money," I say. "I left in a hurry." Never one to overlook the opportunity to add on the vig up front, my sister replies,

"I'll buy you a Curly Wurly, but you'll owe me two back."

"Okay," I say. Not really minding, as tough economics makes the sweet even sweeter. We walk up the road away from the cottage and Gavin Gipson's dad's silent exposure.

Barrow's sweet van is parked on the grass verge of the country lane that leads toward the woods. It is brown and beaten and very old, a relic from the 1940s, and if you believed its owner, Mr. Barrow, it might have done swift trade for the black market during World War Two.

Mr. Barrow is leaning against the van's side, smoking a roll-up with yellowed fingers, listening to a cricket match on a transistor radio held close to his ear. He shakes his head when he sees us, his face wrinkling into a massive smile.

"Botham's taken eight wickets and scored a century to boot . . . in one inning!!!"

"Is that good, Mr. Barrow?"

"GOOD? It's a bloody miracle. Man should be made prime minister. I'll open the van for you girls, but I'm going to keep listening if you don't mind, in case pigs start flying over Nottingham."

He opens the van doors wide throughout his ecstatic cricket-speak, drawing out a scented cloud of heavenly, sweet confection from the windowless cavity inside.

Every inch of the van is covered in sweets. Purpose-built shelves are stacked, like stadium seating, with every chocolate bar imaginable. The inside of the van's doors hold paper bags filled with quarter pounds of various treasures: Sherbet

Lemons, Liquorice Allsorts, Fruit Salads, and Cola Cubes. When there is more time on previous Thursdays, when I'm not on the lam, Kate and I will stand with other kids for maybe an hour, debating the merits of one sweet over another. Do you actually get more candy with a Twix because there are two of them? Is that in fact better than the thicker, more packed investment of a Starbar?

Kate takes two Curly Wurlys, pays Mr. Barrow, and then we stand there just staring at all the chocolate, at the dreamy retrofit of the van itself, its unbeautiful outside and the ingenious display of its delicious center. I could stand there all day but just as I'm realizing that my getaway is unfolding at a fairly leisurely pace, Mum appears around the side of the van.

"What are you doing buying sweets? [Hello, Mr. Barrow.] Put them back immediately and go in the house."

"Why can't we have the sweets? It's Thursday, and it's our money," I say, ill-advisedly doubling down.

"*My* money," says Kate imploringly "And I'm not in trouble." My sister has no qualms about throwing me under the sweet van.

"Put the sweets back, both of you, and go back to the house." Mum is keeping a lid on it for the sake of Mr. Barrow, who is clearly uninterested in our domestic squabbles and is lost in the cricket match.

Kate sadly puts the Curly Wurlys back with the others. I am furious.

"I didn't even do anything wrong."

"You climbed out the window and jumped off the roof."

"I had been imprisoned."

"You had been asked to do math."

"There was no *asking,* there was only *telling,*" I say. My mother sighs mightily.

"He only tells you to do stuff because you won't when he asks."

"The things he wants us to do are to get us out of the way so he can watch the cricket." I am not wrong about this, but there is no way I am going to end up right either.

"Just go and apologize."

"FOR WHAT?"

"For not doing what he said."

I am struck dumb by her reasoning. I watch her question and interrogate everything in her own life, I'd watched her wrest back the power of decision-making from her relationship with my father and now here she is, telling me to "just go" and do what this man says, and worse, apologize to him for doing what she taught me—which was to question.

I am too young and too inexperienced in the nuances of relationships to understand what a tightrope my mother is trying to balance upon. Back in the cottage, at the kitchen table, toolbox spilled out, drill still in hand, my stepfather sits, fuming. He is a small-animal vet and very kind and good with animals, presumably because they don't talk back. My mother looks anxiously at him, then back at us, her daughters—we are still a mystery that she is getting to know. Her love for us is deep and abiding, but the hardwired idea that needing a man is paramount to survival is still acutely present in her. It will be with immense pleasure that as I grow up, I'll watch her shed this idea, like a finely layered cocoon, until she finally emerges, free and empowered. But that's not happening today. Right now, this relationship with this particular man has got to work. And my childlike dislike for his authority, his binary approach to kids, and any kind of emotion, mixed with my sister's careful eggshell walking around everything, are drawing a line in the sand for our mother. Nobody is happy. The uninspired go-to for all parents who are annoyed by children's noncompliance rears its boring head.

"Say you're sorry and then go to your room." My stepfather puts down the drill and looks pointedly at me. I feel the boil of injustice and look to my mother for help, but she can only look down at her feet, and I am marooned on my small island that is turning into more of a volcano.

"I am not sorry about running away from math, but I AM sorry about YOU. You are mean, and—." I don't get the rest of my thought, which I am now yelling, out, before he is up from his seat and has slapped me across my cheek. The silence after it is shocking.

"Go to your room," he says a little sadly, and I turn and go. Kate's eyes are brimming, and my mother is still looking down. I take the stairs two at a time for the second time that day and go straight to the mirror in the bedroom Kate and I share. I stand looking at my face and watch the redness on my cheek take on the shape of a handprint. I am fascinated by the fact that you can see the outline of actual fingers. I pick up a black marker from our small desk and without taking my eyes away from those of my reflection, start to draw around the shape of the slap. It is immediately satisfying, like putting a trophy on a shelf, like tattooing on your body the name of someone you will come to not love.

"You look bananas," says Kate. "I'm very sorry he slapped you."

"I'm not. Now I'm proof." I do not know exactly what I am proof of, it is too complicated to understand completely, but I need proof of something; a way to outwardly define the internal chaos. The black marker on my face feels definitive.

Dinner is a strange affair. There is even less room at the kitchen table tonight and I sit directly across from my stepfather, enjoying his discomfort, as I slowly nod my head up and down, his black-lined handprint waving back at him. Mum asks me to meet her in the garden after dinner and we go to the fruit cage to pick loganberries—they are as if raspberries carried on growing longer than necessary and can cover the whole first joint of your forefinger when worn.

"Min."
"Mum."
"This can't go on."
"I know. He is awful."
"Darling, he is not awful, he's trying. It's hard."
"He slapped me." She stops, looks up at the sky through the wire of the cage.
"I married him. I am married to him."

I know she realizes none of this is ideal, I don't know what she thought it would be, what was so wrong with our other life, I don't yet know about escapes that take you farther than the woods.

"You like school, don't you?" she asks.
"Yes. It's great. I love it."
"Would you like to be a boarder and not have to deal with these dinners?" I should have had the presence of mind to ask if *she* would like not to have to deal with these dinners, but I am only eight and, at the moment, I feel like I am being offered something good.

"Can I come home on weekends?"

"Yes, if you want to."

"Won't it be weird boarding when we only live three miles away from the school? Most of the boarders there live in New York or Yorkshire."

"We can do what we like," she says, now staring at the dark mud we are standing in. "Sort of."

And so I start boarding. It is a terrible mistake. It is in the top three worst mistakes I will ever make, and it'll take many years' time to appreciate and see how much good will actually grow out of it. For all the delight in getting away from confrontation with my stepfather, I realize too late that the collateral damage is having removed myself from the steadying force of my mother. Like an anchor I've previously taken for granted, now that I am cut loose, the drift is unbearable.

My school is a nurturing, deeply connected community, full of creativity and interest. We are free-range children, academics are the mainstay, but they are woven into a much bigger panoply of experience. In simpler terms, I learn to successfully keep bees along with doing my reading comprehensions. But at night, in a large dormitory with seven other girls, I find myself in a ring of hell that Dante somehow missed. It begins with an ache as everyone is brushing their teeth, the knowledge that this part marks the awful creep toward "lights out" and sleep that will never come for me. I try to keep conversations going as long as possible to stave off the inevitable. One by one they all fall asleep, and I am left alone with the ache that now takes up every part of my body. I lie rigid in this new life, which is itself inside a new life. I am so far away from the home we had before, and the home we have now, I'm the smallest one who doesn't open inside a Matryoshka doll.

At 3:00 a.m. one night I race through pitch-black corridors to get to the pay phone, and I call my mother.

"Mama?"

"Min?"

"You have to come and get me; I can't bear it."

"I can't come and get you. It's the middle of the night."

"Of course you can, you just get in the car. I'm down the road!!! Please, Mum, please."

"Darling, you'll get used to it."

"I don't want to get used to feeling awful."

"You wanted to do this."

"Yes, but I got it wrong."

"Well, it'd be no fun for you here, you know that."

"I don't care about fun, I just want—" The phone starts beeping, needing more money that I don't have.

"Please, just come." But she is gone.

Small feet on cold stone, hot tears, as I drag myself back to the dormitory, through the dark hallways, hoping a night monster will get me and then they'll be sorry. I lie in bed and think about running away, but where to? It is a strange feeling to know that while I can make an escape, my destinations have one by one ceased to be places of sanctuary.

That's not to say I don't run away some days. I take off, and wind up back at the cottage; but even as I hang over the garden wall trying to catch my breath, there isn't anything there for me. I watch my mother see me through a window, then stand in the doorway, jangling her car keys, pointing for me to get in the car, I can viscerally feel that the part of her I want—the part that would wrap me in its arms and steady the world again—is gone, or rather is being used to forge this new life. Our agreement on what would make that life happy had bifurcated and we both now drift on our separate, tiny islands of need.

However, the part of school that doesn't involve sleeping is, for the most part, excellent. The headmaster of the lower school is a man named Alastair Langlands. He wears plus fours (a sort of tweed hunting pantaloon), linen shirts, a vest and jacket, and he has a pocket watch. He also has wavy copper hair and smiles most of the time, not in an unstable way, but largely, I feel, because he is constantly delighted by most definitely being in the exact place he wants to be, doing what he loves. He feels like a conflation of characters that several authors could have written: a bit of Thomas Hardy, a lot of Shakespeare, some Dickens, but mostly Chaucer. As the headmaster, the curriculum can be subject to his will. When we study *As You Like It* in English Lit, he provides us with Ordnance Survey maps of the surrounding countryside, splits us into small groups, and tells us to go out and find the Forest of Arden. The idea is that we will all then location scout each group's chosen spot and vote on which place is best. Then we will rehearse the play, invite an audience, and perform the play in our democratically elected forest. He casts me as The Duke, and when I ask him what The Duke is like, he says,

"He is a greedy usurper." I ask him what "usurper" means and he says, "Go to the library and look it up. That is called research." I go, and dutifully report back:

"He doesn't sound very nice."

"He is not. And he ends up a hermit in a cave."

"What is a hermit?"

"Research," he says, pointing back at the library.

It is Sunday night again, and as soon as my mother pulls up to the school to drop me off, I am out of the car and sprinting. I have been saving my money, and my plan is to get to the train station and get on a train to where the woman who had previously been our nanny lives. She is a cross between Maria in *The Sound of Music* (postpostulant, pre-tipping her wimple at Captain Von Trapp) and Mary Poppins. Which basically makes her Julie Andrews. I love her almost as much as my mother. By the time I have streaked across the lower meadow from the playground, I stop to catch my breath and realize that in my haste to run away, I have forgotten the small tin box I'd been keeping my money in. I stop at the edge of some fields and stare around me. I can keep running, but now I don't know where to go. I lean back against a giant oak tree that stands between me and the distance and I try to formulate a plan. I cannot go forward, I certainly cannot go back, and as I hear the voices of people calling out my name, I go up. The tree, having fitted itself to being climbed by schoolchildren for the past eighty years—and who knows whoever else before that—has gnarled knots as strong as a stepladder and a good, smooth first branch from where to get your bearings and choose your ascent. As the voices get closer, I climb faster and soon I'm hidden in the canopy. It is a stroke of luck I think that I am tree-camouflage ready in my "It's Not Easy Being Green" T-shirt and brown corduroy shorts.

From up here I can see my mother walking with Alastair Langlands through the meadow; neither of them looks particularly frantic, as my running off is pretty standard. They know it will be the cold that brings me back; there is no choice between fear of the outside darkness and fear of the inside dormitory darkness, so cold becomes the great leveler. I hear my mum say,

"I'll go back and see if she did a loop and is hiding in

the trunk of the car again." Mum turns to go and there is existential confusion as I watch her walk back up through the meadow, knowing I only want to be with the person I am hiding from. Alastair carries on walking toward me and the tree until he is directly under us. He looks up, smiling, and says,

"You are an excellent climber. I can't actually see you, or know for sure that you are there, but if you are, well done."

I'm not falling for this: the bonhomie, the gentle entreaty, the slow walk back, the long night in sad hell.

"I myself was very homesick as a boy. I understand how awful it feels. I wish that someone had noticed how sad I was, because then I wouldn't have been alone with it. I don't have a cure for what you're feeling, but I do know that it *will* pass, and you're such a good person to have around the place, we would all miss you very much if you left or disappeared up a tree forever. There is a very good book I hope you'll read called *The Baron in the Trees* by Italo Calvino. It's about a man who goes up into the trees near his castle in Italy and never comes down. He lives a very happy life up there. If I don't see you tomorrow in assembly, I will bring the book back and hoist it up to you in a basket. But I hope you do come down, if of course you *are* up there and I'm not just talking to myself. I'm not going to make you come down, and I am certainly not climbing up there, but would you just give me a whistle if you think you might, and I will call off the hounds?"

I don't want to whistle. I don't want anyone to know I hear them, feeling so not heard myself. Alastair pats the trunk of the tree and heads back up toward the school. When he is almost at the gate at the top of the meadow, I stick my thumb and forefinger in my mouth and give the sharp whistle I'd perfected the previous summer.

He turns back and shades his eyes against the sun, which is now setting directly behind the tree.

"That's quite a whistle!" he shouts. I then howl like a wolf to show him it's not all I've got.

Our school is a community. Its motto is "Work of Each for Weal of All." "Weal" comes from the Old English word "wela," meaning well-being. We have as much time outdoors as we do in, and academics are mixed with learning about the land and our responsibility as custodians, and the experience is far more holistic than at most other schools. Word comes in one day that a bypass from the local freeway has been proposed. The bypass will apparently unclog traffic that upsets local taxpayers, and the price for assuaging their impatience is a giant road that will cut through part of our school grounds and destroy a good deal of wild countryside beyond. There is an outcry from people who don't commute to London every day, from people who don't mind a slower pace, who feel that woodlands and long-established ecology are worth protecting from development. Our school is at the forefront of the dissent, and in keeping with its spirit of congenial creativity, our best form of attack (we are told) is to write a protest musical.

I am so into this idea. I really want to be mad at something, and sing. Alastair Langlands and the fourth-grade English teacher, Tom, start writing. The opus they deliver a month later is called "Bypass the Parcel." The title, it is explained, references something called "bureaucracy," while also playing on the word "parcel," which apparently is a measure of land. Once all this has been explained in a special activism assembly, I am impressed by the cleverness of a double meaning and really ready for a sanctioned fight.

The musical is beautifully crafted. Each song illustrates a different part of the argument for and against the road being built. We play staccato singing statisticians, crunching numbers in white coats, spitting out variables of traffic flow and efficiency models, robotic in our processing of the environment. We are irritated businesspeople driving to work in a huff and also carloads of holidaymakers sitting in traffic with screaming kids. We play ourselves—children trying to learn over the roar of traffic, then sadly lamenting the destruction of the homes to all the rabbits and squirrels and badgers and birds. In the dystopian finale, we play the road itself; it's an instrumental, contemporary dance number, and we wear black catsuits and balaclavas. The choreography interlocks us across the stage, growing and spreading like a virus.

There is one solo in the entire musical, and I learn that

anyone who wants to be considered must first audition. I do not know exactly what this means. My friend Greta explains:

"You go and sing a song in front of them and then they say who's the best."

"Why do they get to say who's the best?"

"'Cause they're the choosers."

"What if more than one person is the best?"

"I don't think that's possible."

"But there's got to be more than one brilliant singer?!"

"I dunno."

"It seems weird. It's just what *they* think. Someone else might think something different, so how do you know for sure?"

"I dunno."

Our nine-year-old brains wrestle with the problem of subjectivity and empiricism.

"I thought we weren't supposed to judge each other," I lament.

"But I guess somebody has to," says Greta with a sigh.

We both decide to sign up for the audition, neither one realizing it might be catastrophic for our friendship. I practice my audition song in the tiled shower room, where it sounds really great. I wonder if I could get them to come down here and listen. We stand in line outside the main hall where we have our assemblies, waiting to audition. I hear a boy inside giving "Night Fever" everything he's got. It's a hard song to sing a cappella with a very English accent, and without your brothers backing you up, but he commits to the falsetto with a choir boy's devotion. He gives me a massive thumbs up as he exits, and I go in to find Tom and Alastair sitting behind a table and making notes.

"Hello, Minnie. What are you going to sing for us?"

"'Evergreen,' by Barbra Streisand, from the movie *A Star Is Born*."

"Well, carry on in your own time, and let's see if a star IS born!" beams Alastair.

I don't get it. But I hum my first note to give me a starting point and then launch into this song whose melody I love but whose lyrics are a word salad of incomprehensible meaning. I do know that Christmas trees are evergreens, because we have been learning about the difference between conifers and deciduous trees in science, so that is what I think of as I sing.

"Ageless and evahhhhh, evahhhhhhh greeeeeeeeeeeen."

My eyes are tightly shut, my fists clenched as the song finishes. Alastair and Tom smile in what I hope is appreciation
and not pity.

"Most passionate, Minnie, yes—'morning glory and midnight
sun'—what a way with words Miss Streisand has, excellent,
excellent. Thank you very much, off you go."

I leave and Greta is waiting outside. It's a bit awkward and
for some reason we shake hands.

"Meet you on the swings afterward?" I say. She nods and goes
into the hall as I head out into the playground.

Later, on the swings, Greta says,

"It felt annoying wanting them to like me." I think about how
much I want them to like me but say nothing.

"I wonder what the solo song is about," she muses.

"It's about a tree. It's about the big climbing tree at the
bottom of the meadow," I tell her. I had overheard some
teachers talking the other day about it. The five-hundred-
year-old oak, my running-away tree, would be felled if they
built this road.

"That's terrible."

"It is."

I feel particularly guilty because I would want to sing that solo whether it was about the tree I loved or not. The tree had been singled out for destruction. I just wanted to be singled out.

If given the chance, I would protest my heart out on behalf of that beautiful tree, singing that song, but even more importantly, I would be doing it in front of an audience.

"I would like to save that tree," says Greta.

"I would like to sing that song," I reply.

We sit, razor-straight-backed, in assembly the next day. After some announcements Alastair tells us that they have decided who will sing the solo in the musical. It is me. I feel a flood of good feeling I don't have a single word for. The only comparable experience so far is seeing my mother when she comes to pick me up from school on a Saturday morning. It is a feeling of things being absolutely right, and I am unused to such certainty. Looking around, I see Greta's face crestfallen and stormy, and my fleeting moment of certainty wavers. We speak very little during our morning classes, but at lunchtime, back on the swings, she says:

"You are the best. That's why they picked you." I like the idea of being the best, but I still believe what I'd said to her before.

"I don't think there is only one best. I think there is just the person that they pick."

"And they picked you."

"Yes. This time."

"You're really happy," she says unhappily, "And I'm not. Because of you, but I'm also glad you're happy. It's very confusing that it's not one thing."

"Can't it be both?" I say.

"No. 'Cause that feels like a lie."

"But it's true!"

"I don't want to feel so complicated," she says, jumping lightly off the swing.

"Are we still friends?" I ask her hesitantly.

"I dunno," she replies.

For someone who had been very clear about her discomfort with the murky marriage of opposites, her answer is annoyingly opaque. Everything is two things, I think, or even more than two things. I feel happy and sad about being here at this school, there are people who love the idea of the new road and people who hate it, I am consistently both pissing people off and making them laugh. Why is any of this such a surprise to you, GRETA? I scuff the worn ground at the base of the swing and realize I am late for my first rehearsal of the solo. I pass Greta on my way to the music room; she is with a bunch of kids, planting some herbs in a raised bed by the back of the school kitchen. I wave, and she smiles but doesn't wave back.

Tom is waiting with his guitar in the music room. He is tall and thin, and he has taught me a lot of things already, including sarcasm. There is an ambivalence about him, the feeling that there is always something else he would rather be doing, but he is funny, if a little scary.

"Sorry I'm late."

"No, no. There's nothing I like more than waiting around for kids."

"Sorry."

He smiles and starts playing the song. The melody is very pretty and sweet, the lyrics are a mixture of grandiose sentiment and self-pity, and I am thrilled at having the chance to try and sincerely pull them off.

THEY SAID IT WAS MYYYYY TREE, I CLIMBED
  RIGHT TO THE TOP,
AND MADE THE WHOLE WORLD STOP,

AND LISTEN WHILE I SANG MY SONG,
SUCH A BEAUTIFUL HIIIIIIGH TREE, WITH
   BRANCHES SPREAD SO WIDE,
I'D HIDE MYSELF INSIDE,
WHERE NOTHING COULD GO WRONG.

He plays it a few times and I join in the second time around, clutching my sheet of lyrics. Then like every soloist before me, I have some notes:

"Um. Could we drop the key? I'm having a hard time making the A."

"Oh, *are* you?"

"Yes."

"Well, perhaps if you practiced it a bit, you'd find out how to do it."

"I definitely will practice. But if you dropped it even half a step the high note would be an F and it would just be easier." Tom looks nonplussed.

"Why do you think making it easier is a good thing?" I wonder if this is a trick question or if he really doesn't know the answer.

"Because . . . easier is nicer . . . and not . . . hard?"

"It's good to have to reach for that note a bit, work for it, it'll feel good when you manage to do it."

That was the thing with teachers, they were always teaching.

"But aren't there enough hard things?," I said. "Why can't we make it easier if we already know how to?" Tom looks down at his guitar and picks a bit of fluff off a string

"I'm not dropping the key."

I never figure the note out. It is a strangulated high point of the song and will just have to remain so. I try various ways to get around it, my favorite is acting, like I'm overwhelmed with emotion, and the bum note is just a by-product. Tom rolls his eyes when I do this, but I figure once I'm onstage, he can't very well stop me. The musical comes together in rehearsal and is quite amazing in style, concept, and execution. We are selling tickets for the show to raise money for the protest, and my first taste of creatively opposing something feels righteous.

One afternoon, about a week from our first performance, Alastair stops me in the hallway.

"Hello, hello, how's the big song? I liked it very much when I heard it last, particularly the moment where you appeared full of anguish and almost half spoke the lyric. It made me truly feel for the tree. I wanted to let you know there has been interest from the television program *Nationwide* to come and film you singing the song. It will be a wonderful way of increasing visibility of the protest and should sell some seats. How do you feel about going on television?"

Nationwide is a current affairs show on the BBC that runs after the early evening news and features regional stories. I have never thought about being on TV before, so it takes me a minute to answer Alastair's question.

"Do they pay you?"

"They do not. In this instance you are the news, and they are amplifying you, not employing you."

"I see," I say, recalibrating my expectations. "I think it would be a really good thing to do anyway, wouldn't it? Even if they don't pay me."

"I think so, yes. And I have no doubt there will be many opportunities for you to be paid for your performance services in the future. When you are a grown-up."

I am glad for the vote of confidence.

"Okay, I'll do it. For the tree."

"Excellent," he says, patting my shoulder and hurrying away.

I want to tell Greta, but I'm not sure that she, or any of the other kids in my class, will think it a good thing. There is clearly a mixed response to anyone being singled out for something special, and I don't know how to defend it. I decide to wait to share my big news until Saturday morning when my mother comes to pick me and my sister up.

"Mum, I'm going to be on TV."

"What?" says my mother.

"WHAT?" says Kate.

"For the musical. I'm going to be singing my song on the news." They both start laughing and I immediately feel this is not the correct response.

"It's not funny."

"Oh, darling, we are not laughing *at* you, we are laughing because it's so surprising and GREAT."

"No, I am actually laughing at you," says Kate.

We are driving through the back country lanes, toward our cottage, and the car feels rife with mixed messaging.

"When are you going to be on?"

"Next week, on *Nationwide*."

My sister laughs harder.

"That's not the news! That's where they tell you the cricket pavilion is being replaced and that some old lady from down the road had a miracle birth!"

"It IS the news," I squeak. "It is telling people about the protest and the tree and that they can do something."

"Not news," says Kate, "regional fodder."

"All right, all right, that's enough, chicks. I think this calls for a celebration," says my mother, one hand winding open the sunroof in our tiny Ford Fiesta.

"Can we stand up?" I ask.

"You can. I'll go slowly and don't tell the police."

We stand on the backseat and fit our torsos up, through the sunroof. Mum turns the radio up, and with Blondie blaring through the tinny speakers as our soundtrack, we raise our arms, scream along with "Heart of Glass," get a mouthful of insects, and feel like we are flying.

The day arrives for my television debut. It is stark, cold, and extremely windy. I am wearing my uniform, which is in keeping with the slightly eccentric protocols of my school: a kilt and a baggy, thin, short-sleeved blue shirt. I have added long socks, which disappointingly don't quite cover my scabby knees, and wear my least scuffed shoes. The film crew arrives, and they are less glamorous than I had imagined. I had sort of been picturing Farrah Fawcett–type women, but the three men who show up are tired Basil Fawltys. There are a director, a cameraman, and a sound guy, and they clearly want to get the job done as fast as possible.

"Right, where's this tree then?" asks the director. Alastair and Tom (who is wearing his guitar) lead the crew down the meadow to the tree. We stand in what is now a howling gale and the director shouts,

"Can you climb up it?!"
    "Yes!" I shout back.
    "Okay, mic her up, Steve!"

The sound guy threads the cable down the back of my shirt and affixes the radio mic to my collar and the battery pack to my kilt. It's starting to feel a lot more glamorous.

"Okay. Up you go, then!" he roars.

I turn to Tom and Alastair, and they give me four thumbs up. Climbing the tree, I am glad I'm the one singing this song. I feel our fates are intertwined, this tree being the seat and shelter for my own ongoing protest. I'm also pretty sure the wind is going to mask the strangled high note. I sit on the lowest branch, legs dangling, hair plastered across my face, and look down beatifically on the five men.

"Don't worry," I scream. "I'll sing really loudly!"

The school lets me go home a few nights later, to watch *Nation-wide* with my mum and Kate. I feel sick as the graphics signal the beginning of the show. Mum squeezes my arm.

"It's so *exciting,* Min, you're on TV!"

"Let's see if she made the final cut," says my sister. "You never know, she might have been replaced by a crashed milk truck."

Suddenly the anchor is introducing the segment and there is Tom, a shaggy-haired Pete Seeger, strumming the opening chords to the song. The camera begins on a close-up of his fingers on the strings, then cuts to my shoes and pans up my socks, past my scabby knees, and settles on a close-up of my face, which is barely visible through the thicket of hair.

"Not even sure that's you," wheezes Kate through uncontrollable laughter.

"I had to decide," I mumble, "whether to hold onto the tree or my hair." The camera widens to capture just the tree branch and me and you can definitely see my white-knuckled grip. A gust of wind mercifully blows my hair back and we are now appraised of my face in full throws of the song, cheeks almost rippling in the wind tunnel.

"Goodness," says my mother, "you're really giving it your all, aren't you?"

The camera widens out even farther and the strange scene is revealed in full: Tom, leaning into the wind at a forty-five-degree angle and me bellowing the song out, hanging onto the tree for dear life.

"Anyone who turns their TV on at this exact moment is going to be really confused," says my sister.

On the day when we are walking back up to the school having finished filming, Alastair walks beside me.

"Well done for hanging on," he says kindly, "through wind and storm, you prevailed. I think that will make jolly good television. The stage production will most likely be a lot less tempestuous."

A few days later we open the show to a packed house. The charming, pastoral idea of children singing in a school musical is brilliantly overthrown by the reality of children singing to battle the folly of adults. The shameful message of greed and expedience destroying the environment is more keenly delivered because the lyrics are clever and the music catchy and because we are kids. We raise a lot of money over the next week of performances and the captain of the football team pats me on the head and tells me I'm a superstar. I cannot separate the powerful feeling of effecting change with being acknowledged as a performer. Understanding the conflation of responses, both my own and others, will be a knot I will struggle to unpick for the rest of my life.

They didn't build the road. Or at least, not right away. The countryside and the tree had twelve more years of growth and peace before the commuters got their way, and by that time I had left the school with a perfectly imprinted memory of how it used to be. My son now goes to the same school, and when I wander down to that part of the grounds and stand by the freeway siding, I sing the song to myself, in protest of whatever currently needs protesting in my life, and you can't hear a word over the roar of traffic, but I know I am singing.

2

I'M GOING TO MIAMI

I am eleven, and it is the summer. My sister and I have been staying in Barbados with our father and his new girlfriend, the first woman Dad has brought home since our mother left him. Our house is missing an entire wall on one side, allowing the outside to be inside and vice versa—a free-flowing swirl of sea breeze, mango, and dark, sugary earth. When there is a hurricane, a wall gets rolled in on tracks, affixed, and then rattles through the storm, reminding us of its and our impermanence.

It has been a week of gently boiling temperatures and tension. Having no reference with which to metabolize my dad's new girlfriend, I have figuratively been throwing up on her all week. She, unused to children, probably just wanting to hang out with her boyfriend and not his overly articulate kids, has had a pretty hard time. The question attack is a particular favorite of mine:

"Are you sleeping in the spare room or in Dad's room?"

"How long are you planning on staying?"

"Are you twenty years younger than him or thirty?"

"Are you sad our hair gave you lice?"

One afternoon after a stealth insurgence on my part that puts her hair, glasses, and choice of bikini squarely in my sights, she has retreated to the pool. Unable to resist, I head down there to find her.

It's strange to so keenly remember its aftermath, while the battle itself remains hazy. I see my father's face after the fight we had, and the subsequent events his wrath incurred, but I don't really remember what I said to his poor girlfriend, who had unwittingly become a major player in our historic drama.

I stand opposite my father, we are both squared off and bullish, ready for a fight. Our energetic symmetry would be funny if we could see it.

"This is my house, not her house. This is our vacation, not her vacation. You are my dad, not hers."

My father's face moves through stages of slowly solidifying concrete from the beginning of this fight till the end.

"It is actually my house and you will be polite to anyone I invite into it."

"It is OUR house, then. WE staked out the foundation. I remember doing the orange tape. There is a photograph of us doing it. THERE IS PROOF."

My father stands very still when he is angry and forced to deal with emotion. I always describe him as bear-like, but he is really a cat. A big, scary cat.

"You will go and apologize to her immediately. You shouted at her and that is unforgivable."

"I shouted because nobody listens to me."

"You told her to leave."

"I told her to go to the beach if all she was ever going to wear was a bikini, even to dinner."

"Who on EARTH are you to tell anyone anything? You are utterly insufferable. Go and apologize."

"I will not."

And with that, the concrete sets, and my last retort is, indeed, my last retort.

"Very well," says my father. "That's it. Get out of my sight. And you will be put on the next plane back to England."

It is grim staring at concrete, concrete you knew you were mixing even as you wished you weren't.

"Go to your room."

These particular words should really be my epitaph. Though I never realized it throughout my childhood, they are the condemnation from which all my adventures will spring; the apparent finality and incarceration will give me something to break free and run from. They are actually extremely creative words in disguise. At eleven, though, it is too good a disguise for me to see through.

I slope off to my room, which immediately shape-shifts into a cell. I hear my father shouting at his assistant to book a flight. I hear my sister pleading with Dad and also being shouted at. Everyone who hasn't really upset him got shouted at, you only really knew you were in trouble when he didn't raise his voice. I sit on my bed, heart thumping, wondering why I can't apologize. My door isn't locked, but I stay where I've been told to go and watch the shadow lengthen slightly on the guava tree outside my window.

Eventually my sister brings me a mango.

"You should probably pack, Min."

"Really? He's not really going to send me away, is he?"

"Yeah. He is." If my dad is a cat, then my sister is a sphinx. Cat adjacent, very mysterious. She leans in the doorway, then reaches up to get my suitcase down from the top of the closet.

"You've really done it now," she says, extremely equably.

"Why?"

"The girlfriend started sobbing when Dad went to see if she was all right."

"Why does that mean I've got to go?"

Kate pauses while folding T-shirts and putting them in my case.

"Dunno. There has to be a payment, I guess. Quid pro sobbing." My sister is always a calm presence in all my getting-sent-aways. Never for a second does she point out that when I go, she is left ostensibly alone.

"The car's coming in an hour." This strikes me as strange

because there is only one flight for England, and it is a night flight. Right now it is most certainly still barely afternoon.

"Why am I going so early? Will I just sit at the airport till the evening?"

"I dunno, Min," she says a bit sadly. Then, perking up considerably, she says,

"Oooooo, get me duty-free perfume. Dad never lets me 'cause he says it makes me smell like a tart's window box. I'll give you money."

"Okay." I feel awful leaving her. "Sorry, Bates."

"It's okay. Her bikini is kind of pretty though."

"Yeah," I say. "But when she bends over to pick something up you can basically see what she had for breakfast."

"You've heard Dad say that about other people."

"Yeah. Dunno why it would piss him off so much then."

None of it makes any sense. There is no conversation about all this change. New people wander into our landscape and nobody but me thinks it's weird. No one interrogates the motives of the interlopers but me, and now apparently this is a punishable offense.

I am standing under the peacock flower tree in our driveway. Its bright red flowers offer a cheerful canopy to my doom. My dad's assistant, John, stands by the door of the house and a waiting taxi chugs. Its driver fiddles with the radio: reggae to soca and back to reggae. He hasn't even turned the engine off. He knows this will be a quick good-bye. I think he has picked me up before, but that time it was only to drive me across the island to stay with our friends Jack and Margaret, while Dad cooled down.

John is a kind, middle-aged American man. A figure whose default setting is to dart around, dealing with both my father's business concerns and personal ones. I think, though, even by his extremely helpful, organized standards, it is odd for him to be telling me what he now tells me.

"So, uh, listen. There's a little snafu on the old travel itinerary. It seems the flight to England is booked solid tonight so, ah, you're not going on that flight."

"Am I staying, then?"

"No. You're going."

"Where am I going?"

"Well, ah, you see . . . uh, you're gonna take a flight to Miami, stay there for a night and a day at the Fontainebleau Hotel, then get on the flight tomorrow evening to London."

"Who's going with me?"

"Well, uh, well, yeah, um, no one." The breeze ruffling the red flowers of the tree above me blows harder—suddenly a sharp wind. The tree, my chorus, gasps.

I have always been able to cry very easily, it will be a useful tool as an actress, but as a child I use it rather too often for people to take the emotion behind the crying (or lack thereof) very seriously. The tears that now prickle the back of my eyes, the tightness in my throat, feel private and unwanted; I don't want to share them and now they are using me rather than the other way around. I have never been anywhere by myself; I am a pack animal who might have dreamed of their own hunt but would never actually creep out of the cave to do it.

"Don't worry," John says nervously, "you'll be looked after at the airport and on the plane and then a driver will pick you up in Miami and take you to the hotel. There might be a big sign with your name on it," he said unconvincingly. He then lit a cigarette, which I knew was a bad sign as he'd very publicly quit a few weeks before.

"It's great, the Fontainebleau, it's got this crazy staircase that goes nowhere. It's called 'The Staircase to Nowhere.'"

That sounds about right, I think, as my sister appears at the door.

"'Bye, Minnow. Don't forget to have a club sandwich by the pool."

My sister and I are very fond of club sandwiches: another layer of toast . . . *inside*?? We swoon every time we eat them, marveling at their height and just how much you can pack into one sandwich. They are a marvel, and by our reckoning of sandwich physics, without stabilizing crusts—shouldn't really be able to stand up. The thought cheers me considerably.

"Don't forget to take the toothpick out!" she calls as I get into the car. *Of course*, I remember—that *is how they stay standing up*. I wave out of the window for as long as I can see her, then the car turns onto the road, and suddenly I am really gone.

I love sitting in the backseat of cars. As the youngest, it is automatic relegation, but I don't mind because to me the backseat is where all the good things happen. I often roll down the window and stick my head out; wind whipping my hair back feels delicious, as my hair usually wraps around my head like a vine and obscures pretty much everything.

Growing up in Barbados, there is just one main road from the west to the south, where the airport is. It is all cane fields and small cottages, with an occasional rum shop. There are also quite a lot of road-based cricket matches, so any journey on this road is usually broken up if a particularly fast bowl catches the driver's attention and we have to pull over and wait to see if the wicket is struck or just how far the ball is thwacked. I take long, deep breaths as we pass a rum factory; deep, sweet air from the boiling sugar, green towers of newly cut cane and steam rising from the chimney. I snap my eyes shut and open them, making a clicking sound as I do it. This is how I have always taken my pictures; I store them away, each frame returned to in memory through the long, cold winters in England. Squinting over the fields, I can just make out the sea, which I now realize I have not said good-bye to. I hadn't said good-bye to my father either, but frankly I am sadder about the sea. Usually before I leave the island I swim out at the beach nearest our house, dive down as far as I can, and yell a gurgling salutation/lament that serves as an indication I will return. I feel bereft of proper good-byes. Tears are now clearly visible, which prompts the driver to speak to me for the first time.

"Don't cry in the back of my car, it's bad luck." He then turns the radio up and gives me a thumbs up through the rearview mirror.

"Reggae'll make you right."

We arrive at the airport, which is a steamy block of beige concrete full of tourists who don't want to leave. I feel comforted. A woman from the airport has clearly been looking out for us and flags down the taxi.

"Cheer up, chicken," the driver says as I get out.

"Feel good. Feel free." He has one gold tooth that is smaller than all the rest and it flashes in the light as he smiles at me. He revs the engine, accelerates fast, and twenty feet later screeches to a halt to pick up a glut of holidaymakers who then squash into the good vibes of his backseat.

The woman from the airport, whose name is Ronky, gets me through passport control and gives me a Fanta. It is a twelve-ouncer, the kind I was never allowed. Things were looking up.

"You gotta wear this tag around your neck," she says, "so if you get lost, you'll know who you are." I don't query the logic because she lights a Kool with an air of great authority and puts the tag around my neck.

"Can I go to duty-free?"

"Yes, sugar, but come right back here and don't try to buy

any cigarettes." She winks, and I feel like we are pals. I now want to buy cigarettes, but I want to give them to her.

I go to the duty-free and find "Charlie: The Gorgeous Sexy Fragrance. By Revlon." My sister will be thrilled.

"Can I get a carton of Kool cigarettes, please?" I ask the man at the counter.

"No."

"They're for my friend?"

"Can't do it, child. Can't do it. And smoking is not Kool." He air-quotes the word as he says it, and smiles, to let me know it's a joke. I don't think it's that funny, but I know my sister will when I tell her, so I laugh way louder than necessary. Back in the arctic air-conditioning of the lounge I sit down where Ronky had left me and look around for her.

I always want grown-ups to like me but find it difficult to behave in a way that seems to consistently please them. Grown-up love appears to be very conditional, and they are not conditions I can really abide by—not for long, anyway. One minute they're laughing at the fact that I know what "existential" means and the next moment they're all "Can you shut up now? You're really getting on my nerves." I feel like the problem really lies with them, that all the rules they have are made up as they go along, that a couple of drinks or a bad night's sleep will engender a totally new set of expectations from them. It must be hard for them to keep up with their ever-changing opinions. It must be hard to keep redrawing the lines of their own boundaries. It's part of why I like them; I rather pity them.

Ronky seems like a straight shooter, and I think her braids are beautiful. They have wooden beads at the end of them, which I know are made from coconut shell. I stare over at the families gathering for the flight to Miami. White tourists with cornrowed hair; scalps burned in livid, hot pink partitions; plastic beads at the ends of their braids, in sherbet colors of the Caribbean sunset. These women (and some men), unused to their appropriated hairdos, wince as the beads swing every time they turn their heads, thwacking them in the face.

"Pan Am Flight 222 to Miami, now boarding at gate four." The tourists move as one, gathering up their bags of Mount Gay rum and their children in a heave of mismatched tan lines. I feel a lurch of worry. I don't know what to do now. It is just me and a bottle of Charlie perfume stuffed in a canvas bag along with the small blanket I always sleep with, and a book about penguins. But there, through the throng, I see Ronky swaying toward me, smiling and unhurried, waving my boarding pass as a hello, even though it is really good-bye.

Sitting on the plane, I do everything they tell me to: I fasten my seat belt, check the exits, eat the peanuts. I am in the middle seat with a man sitting next to the window and a woman on the aisle. She finishes off the rum and Coke she'd brought with her from the lounge and is asleep before takeoff. Sandwiched between them, I feel a rush of panic as the plane gathers speed along the runway.

"Excuse me, sir, but we are definitely going to Miami,

aren't we?" The man nods, looking out the window. "Yup. That is where we are going." It is strange to feel relief that I am indeed on the right plane, going to a place I don't want to go to.

"Why you going there?" he says. "You on vacation?"

I pause before answering because, what was I on? There wasn't a word for it in my lexicon of either travel or transgression. I think it best to stick to the facts so I tell him,

"I'm on my way to England."

"England? Hoooo. That place cold and dark." He shivers at the thought. "Solid cricket, though, and I do love it when the West Indies crush them like a cockroach." I am suddenly aware that I am heading into a conversation about which I know nothing at all. I do what my father does when this happens.

"Yes, indeed," I say.

"Would you excuse me?" I then turn my head from him rather slowly and look forward at the seat in front of me. This would have to serve as a polite exit, as the rum and Coke lady is asleep on her tray table. The man chuckles and puts his Walkman headphones on.

"You are excused."

Perhaps it is this first moment of being truly alone. Perhaps before, I couldn't see the plane for the clouds and the noise of so many others in my tribe; but now, flying with no one but myself, I discover a feeling of freedom and a realization that I love being in transit.

It is an existential corridor where I'm not tethered to who I was on departure or who I'll be when I land. The pressure of expectation is released. That's not to say I want to run naked down the aisle and grab a drinks trolley from the galley, but rather that all the myriad interactions with life are put on hold. It is the relaxation of an exhale of a pause. I am anyone here.

I look around at all the people on the plane being quiet or noisy distillations of themselves. Adults are very childlike it seems when they think no one is looking: laughing out loud at books, picking their noses, singing along to the music in their headphones. I imagine briefly what would happen if they let go of the rule-making and rule-abiding more permanently; if they felt and said what they thought and didn't punish anyone who saw it differently. I appreciate that it would be child-led chaos, and then rather contrarily, think that I can't wait to grow up and stay a child.

As we eat the food that is served, I really want to tell the woman next to me to *have* the ice cream she clearly wanted but emphatically declined. Nobody who doesn't want ice cream says no to it that hard. The flight attendant had said:

"Ma'am, would you like some ice cream?"

"ICE CREAM? . . . GOD, NO . . . . JESUS . . . NO, NO, NO! I REALLY COULDN'T POSSIBLY EVEN THINK ABOUT IT."

I'd asked if I could have hers—this being an existential corridor.

"Are you sure it won't give you a tummyache, sweetheart?" says the nice flight attendant. "You have had quite a lot already."

"I doubt it will," I say, "but there is a loo nearby, isn't there?" The nice flight attendant nods her head uneasily.

Lulled into a faux sense of not being, the crackle of the intercom and the pilot's voice announcing our descent come as a physical jolt. As my ears begin to pop, I wonder if the dread I was beginning to feel had been waiting here for me all along; having hopped on an earlier flight, had it just been hanging around in the etheric lounge, waiting for me to catch up?

Moments before, we had all been in the same suspension. Now, as people began to straighten their clothes and put away their playthings, life and duty were starting to rematerialize. I would have liked to stay on that plane. Perhaps indefinitely.

"See ya later, princess," says the man sitting next to me, as he stands and grabs his bag from the overhead locker. He has listened to music the entire flight and shouts his good-bye over the tinny buzz coming from his headphones.

"Good-bye, Mr. Music," I mouth without speaking. What was the point? He couldn't hear me, and also, who knew what social contracts had been dispensed with while we were in the air?

The nice flight attendant stands with me in the galley and

holds my hand as all the other passengers disembark. With the last whiff of Coppertone and body odor disappearing up the gangway, a heavily accessorized matron is revealed standing at the entrance to the aircraft. Her enormous bosom is tucked neatly into the waistband of her skirt, and she offers a hand that has a ring on every finger.

"Hi Minnie Mouse I'm Margot Special Greeter did you have a nice flight? Thanks Suzanne I got it from here come on now let's hustle." She speaks without taking a breath, leaving no room for response, which I could only suppose saved time.

We move at a clipped pace through the airport. Margot Special Greeter, in very high heels, tips slightly forward as she walks, like someone tripping who is only saved from falling by the momentum of moving forward. This forward thrust finally ends when her hands hit the handle of the trolley in baggage claim. I feel relieved. Watching her swing my suitcase up and off the conveyer belt, I marvel at what women manage to do without complaint, negotiating the world while top-heavy and in heels. I wonder what I will grow into: someone who puts everything on display in a bikini or someone who remains armored with clothes. Did you have to choose what kind of butterfly you emerged as? I hoped I would not be a butterfly with giant boobs, as, any way you sliced it, they seemed to be things that required a lot of thought and accommodation. They seemed almost as troublesome as the big emotions I already knew I had.

We emerge into thick, soupy Miami humidity. Margot Special Greeter bustles me into a cab, puts my bag into the trunk, and tells the cabdriver to take me to the Fontainebleau Hotel.

"I'll see you tomorrow night to put you on the plane to England have fun and order the shoestring fries at the hotel they're just to die for and don't forget to get the Thousand Island dressing on the side." It really was amazing how she said it all in just one breath. I wave as we pull away, she waves back, then turns and launches herself into the curbside crowd.

It is evening now. The heat of the day has settled into the concrete and there isn't so much as a breath of a breeze as we cross Biscayne Bay into Miami Beach. I am quite surprised it isn't actually a beach. Why wasn't it called Miami Island? I ask the cabdriver. He shrugs.

"'Beach' sounds like a place you wanna go to, 'island' is somewhere you got to get away from. *Soy Cubano. Lo sé.*"

Everyone was clearly trying to make sense of it all. I was beginning to see that the greatest difference between adults and children was that they had to provide answers whereas we could just ask questions. Imagine having to know everything. It felt like a burden I couldn't imagine ever wanting. Also, answers felt so finite; they left no possibility of a surprise ending—they closed the door that a question had opened. I really liked asking questions and always enjoyed the conversations they elicited more than the answer. I would have liked to have had the conversation with my father about why he needed to send me away. I didn't need to know the actual reason per se, I just wanted to hear the question out loud and see what he did with it. Maybe he had some questions of his own, maybe if he asked a few more of them out loud, the questions themselves would interrogate the reality, giving it context and the space to settle. Maybe then he wouldn't have had to come up with answers that left both of us so far away from each other.

We pull into the sweeping semicircular driveway of the Fontainebleau Hotel, the driver deposits me at the steps, says adios, and takes off into the night. I'm extraordinarily tired now; having spent a day not being able to escape their grasp, I would now have quite liked an adult's hand to hold. Making my way into the giant lobby, I am struck by the enormous number of people milling about. Everyone is smoking and drinking, women chucking their heads back and laughing like Joan Collins in the Cinzano commercials; men with too whitened teeth and indoor sunglasses lounge, while the women stand. I shuffle through the endless seating areas to what looks like a check-in desk and a man with the biggest hair I've ever seen on a man peers over the edge of the counter.

"Hi, honey, are you lost?"

"I don't think so. I think I'm supposed to be staying here."

"Darlene," he calls over his shoulder, "we've got a little lost kid."

What if the only people who know I am supposed to be here are asleep a thousand miles away? What if to these people here, I am actually lost. I grip the handle of my bag.

"I'm not lost. I'm supposed to be here."

"What's your name, sweetheart?" A woman approaches from the other end of the counter. Her hair, staggering in height and width, seems to be on a delay and doesn't stop swaying until thirty seconds after she's reached the man's side.

"I'm Minnie Driver and my dad said I'm staying here."

"Well, where is your dad, honey? Has he already checked in?"

I find out at this point that it's the more innocuous questions in life that will make me cry. Hard questions in a difficult situation will act as an alloy, they'll make me stronger. It's the soft questions that have no heat behind them, they're the ones that will be my undoing, particularly in public. Towering-haired Darlene with her gentle assumptions—that my dad must be here somewhere, getting ready to welcome me, getting the bags from the car, using the bathroom after a long journey— now benignly jabs through the reality of my situation and into my heart.

She comes flying around the desk, hair bringing up the rear, and is crouching down next to me in seconds.

"Oh, sweetie, don't cry, it's okay, we'll find him, you're okay, I promise you're okay." Through my tears I look at this woman. She doesn't know me, my tears are new for her, no one is forcing her to be kind, though, and she is telling me I am okay and not lost, two things she thinks are true, because she is clearly a nice person and doesn't know that a tougher line of questioning would stop me crying immediately. I am going to have to break it to her that she isn't going to find my dad. And getting into that whole thing with her feels exhausting. I sniff mightily and say,

"There's probably a reservation for me under his name, it's only for a night, I'm just on my way home to England."

"So you're not here with anyone? It's just you, by yourself?" I feel the good old steel start to return.

"Yes. Just me."

"You're here *all by yourself*?" I am standing taller in the face of her consternation.

"Yes."

It is Darlene's turn to tear up. Her lips and her hair wobble.

"Well, goodness me. Goodness me, what a thing. Marshall? Will you look for a reservation under a . . . Mr. Driver, is it?" I nod.

"Here it is," calls Marshall from over the counter. "And there's a credit card on file for incidentals."

Darlene stands, smooths her skirt, and shakes her head slowly as she takes the room key from Marshall. She leads me over to the elevator and we ride it up to the ninth floor. Her eyes, never leaving me, are full of pity, which makes me smile at her somewhat creepily. The room looks out over the enormous pool deck and the Atlantic. I know that straight ahead of me are the Bahamas and that if you followed those islands down, curved to the right, and carried on down and down through the Caribbean, eventually you would hit Barbados, and if you missed it, eventually you would dead-end in Venezuela. I stand in the hotel room with this stranger, looking back at where I'd come from. Almost another life.

"Okay, honey, listen, lock the door after I leave and I'll be back on the front desk at nine o'clock tomorrow morning if you need me. Marshall's there all night if you need to call and speak to a grown-up. Anything you want, just charge it to the room. You be okay?"

"Sure," I say, because I know that's what she wants to hear. And because I am so tired now, I am running out of ways to make grown-ups feel better.

I pull my blanket out of my bag, put my penguin book on the nightstand, kick off my sandals, and get into bed. For the first time in my life, I do not brush my teeth. I wonder if anything significant will happen because of this: Is this the beginning

of the slippery slope I'd always been warned about? I feel myself sliding down it as I fall asleep: a steep, silky slope made of
sugarcane and seawater, sliding down past all the island chains
until finally free-falling the last few feet into my bed at home
in Barbados.

I wake up the next morning, still very much in Miami. My
rather pedestrian dream of being asleep in my own bed at home
disappears as my eyes open and, in its place, rage blooms. Who
lets a child fly by themself to a foreign city where nobody
knows them, and nobody puts them to bed or makes them
brush their teeth? Who leaves a child alone in a hotel? Who
chooses bikinis over blood? The person who'd left his credit
card on file, that's who. I pick up the telephone next to the bed
and press the button that says room service.

"Hello? Can I have some breakfast, please? Thank you.
Can you tell me what is very expensive on your menu? . . .
I'll have that then, without the champagne. And I would also
like the Mickey Mouse pancakes with bacon and a strawberry
yogurt, and a club sandwich and shoestring fries with Thousand Island dressing on the side. Thank you very much." The
room service voice asks me how many people it will be for,
and I feel the sad tide rise for a second.

"No, it's actually just for one person." The tide recedes, and
I hang up the phone. There is no one to stop me from doing
anything I want, or to stop me from crying or to soothe me
if I do. I wonder if I am adventurous enough to do something

really bad; I have never had the opportunity or motive before, but the idea feels ripe for exploration.

I wander over to the window and look at the giant pool deck below and see that people are already setting up shop for a day's lounging. I will eat my breakfast and go for a swim, I think. I will order five lunches and feed them to the seagulls. I will look for opportunities for revenge. I am not entirely sure if you can take revenge on a person without them being present, but I am willing to give it a shot.

Breakfast arrives, wheeled in on a table that, when its hinged flaps are deployed, could easily have seated six.

"Where would you like the table, miss?"

"Over by the window, please."

"Shall I pour the passion fruit juice?"

"Yes, please." He whips out a champagne flute and fills it up.

"You can pretend it's champagne," he says.

"I guess," I reply.

He smiles and play-punches my arm. I think word must have gotten out that there is a stray child in the hotel. Not being particularly manipulative, I am unwilling to trade on being pitied. I am, however, willing to push the boundaries of who I had previously been before being sent to Floridian purgatory. If, in this new world order, I could be dispatched into the unknown, then the person I now was—similarly unknown—should definitely be explored. Maybe she is cool. Maybe she answers back less.

The gentleman who'd brought breakfast leaves after I sign the bill. It had taken rather a long time, as this was a first and I wanted my signature to carry weight. He'd shifted from foot to foot a few times through my laborious cursive but seemed to understand that this was some kind of a moment for me.

"Good job," he said before he took off. Whether it was the curlicue handwriting or the large tip he was referring to, I'll never know. I eat two Mickey Mouse pancakes and the strawberry yogurt and stare regretfully at the mountain of other food. It is a terrible waste, and the sad collateral of revenge takes the shape of a perfect, uneaten club sandwich. This day is moving in one direction, however, and even though I'm planning to spend most of it poolside, there is more revenge business to be done first.

The elevator takes me down to the lobby and there across its sprawling hospitality, I spy the gift shop.

When my father traveled, he would often bring us back presents; they mostly came from the gift shops of the hotels he stayed in. My understanding of these places was that they were probably the most fabulous shops on earth. I have never loved material objects more than those my father gave me when he returned from a trip: a doll with a skirt that turned inside out when you flipped the thing upside down, revealing—another doll with a skirt! (She obviously had no feet and two heads, but she was my kind of exception.) He once brought me a snow globe of the Kremlin where the snow was actually gray, not white; it looked like a bitter thing, and I loved it. Sometimes the gifts would be shiny, beads or glitter attached to plastic in different forms. All of it was treasure, all of it made gift shops an idealized repository of my spangled, candy dreams. And yet, as I both literally and figuratively step into the gift shop of the Fontainebleau Hotel, and cross the threshold of my dreamscape, I do not think twice about co-opting my dream for the purpose of revenge.

I am welcomed by the smell of a thousand scented candles. There is no competition—vanilla always wins. I see the sunglasses tree just where it should be. There are the visors and T-shirts and mugs and dolls: big-haired Barbie knockoffs in a variety of ethnicities, all wearing acid-washed booty shorts and roller skates. They have been positioned in action stances and leer monstrously with rictus grins. They are unbelievable. Fantastic. I take four.

"You need a basket, honey?" says the gift shop man.

"Oh, yes," I reply.

Baskets are a brilliant sales tactic: their usefulness is the decoy to their darker purpose of temptation. Truly, an empty shopping basket is the devil's work, and I walk around the shop, filling mine. The glut filled the emptiness. Napkins printed with palm trees, and flamingo-themed kitchenware I think will be good for my mum, and a lot of dolphin stuff for my sister. I eventually stagger to the counter.

"Phew-ee! You're gonna need another suitcase to fit all that in," says the man. He is right and I ask him if he has any. He points to the wall behind him, upon which are pinned a variety of big-ticket items: a splayed, fluffy toweling robe, a large canvas hold-all, his and hers tennis outfits, and a golf bag, all embroidered with the Fontainebleau's name. These were the things you didn't browse to buy. You were going to make the guy go into the back to get them, so you really needed to intend to purchase. Which I did.

"Can I get everything but the golf bag, please?" The man pauses.

"You're gonna need two of the Hold-All bags to fit all this; you Christmas shopping, honey?"

"No."

"Your parents know you're here?"

"Oh, yes."

"Well, all right." He shuffles off into the back and returns a few minutes later with his arms full.

"That's an awful lot of stuff," he says, looking ruefully at the mountain before him.

"Yeah," I say. "It is."

"How you gonna pay for it?"

"I'm charging it to the room. My dad left a credit card for incidentals."

"You sure he didn't mean toothpaste?"

I fish out a box of Colgate from the pile and brandish it triumphantly.

"Well, all right." He begins ringing it all up and I pull the robe, flip-flops, a baseball cap, some sunglasses, and sunscreen off to one side.

"I'm going to use these now," I said. "Do you think it's possible someone could help me take all the rest up to my room?"

"Yes, honey, sure." He thinks I'm spoiled; I can hear it in his voice, see it in his eyes. "I'll have the bellhop take it all up."

I could have explained it all to him, but I judge him for judging me and decide not to. This punishment of mine is becoming multifaceted. I sign the bill with another laborious signature, shrug off what I don't realize is shame, and head for the pool.

Wherever possible, when there's likelihood of water being present, hot or cold weather, fancy party or picnic—I will wear a swimsuit under my clothes. It starts out as a practicality when you grow up part of the time in a hot country. It ends up being comforting. If there's the ocean or a river or a pool, I will always be able to find a way to excuse myself and jump in. People don't think you're trying to get away from them when you go for a swim. They think you're healthy, strong, secure in how your body looks stripped down. If the weather is cold or raining, they think you're brave. They do not know that water is my escape hatch, the perfect distraction from my anxiety in the shape of a cool gesture.

I have my swimsuit under my shorts and T-shirt, but I find a bathroom where I can take them off and put on the toweling robe I've just bought. I like that the robe has the name of the hotel embroidered on the pocket; it makes me look like I belong. I put on the hat, and the sunglasses, which have a handy, detachable nose guard—it gives the impression I've grown a beak or had recent surgery. I feel pretty good. Armed with sunscreen and my book about penguins, I push through the heavy doors and out into the day.

The pool deck at the Fontainebleau Hotel is ridiculously impressive. It's enormous. You've seen it in lots of movies. Probably most famously in *Goldfinger*, where the eponymous villain plays cards with Bond in the sweltering heat. In 1981 it is essentially miles of concrete with a giant pool in the middle, flanked by a two-level, curving balustrade that faces out toward the Atlantic. There are cabanas built into the balustrade and no umbrellas poolside—presumably to get you to rent a cabana. I walk across the deck toward the rows of sun loungers by the pool, heat pulsing up from the concrete, through my new flip-flops. The fact that the pool is entirely surrounded by concrete cabanas, in a structure high enough so that you can't see the ocean, gives an odd feeling of enclosure. An echoey sun trap. A brutalist playpen. I don't know if it is the architecture or my slightly dour state of mind, but I feel assaulted from every angle by amplified fun. I sit down on a sun lounger and watch as a whole family next to me laugh and roast together.

I look around and see an almost identical family on the other side of the pool doing the same. Vacation symmetry. Everyone subscribing to the same itinerary. The question arises: What are you supposed to do in a collective when you are alone?

I take off my robe and my hat and my beak and I jump into the water. Chlorine will have a pretty good go at ruining any swim; not having goggles while swimming in chlorine comes a close second. But I am not to be deterred. I have a strange realization, once I am in the water, though, that as there is no one to play with, I will just have to swim. Not swimming to get the ball or to dive down to get pennies my mum had thrown in for me and my sister to retrieve, but normal swimming, like grown-ups do. I set off, not sure of the point. My mother is a great swimmer. A champion at school and then later, an elegant sylph, moving effortlessly from front stroke to back, managing to maintain whole conversations while she went up and down and up and down. I swim a few lengths, it feels directionless, which then feels sad. It is disorientating to be sad in an environment in which I am used to being happy.

The pool is largely populated by adults holding drinks; few of the adults are actually swimming.

Women sit on the edge with their legs dangling in the water while their children scream "MOM! Watch THIS" and then proceed to perform no particular feat beyond splashing around, illustrating something I have always known, which is that 90 percent of good parenting is bearing witness.

I get out of the pool, robe-up, and pull my hat down hard on my head. I feel a rising anger that there is yet another by-product of this punishment: making the familiar unfamiliar; making it unsafe. Could all the good things in my life, with the removal of a few key elements, just become ghosts? I suddenly feel very hot in my robe, but it is solid armor, so I will not take it off. The sun is directly overhead now, and I long for someone to tell me to go inside and drink a glass of water and help cut up the christophene for lunch. I need shade. I grab my things and make a beeline for an attendant standing by the nearest cabanas.

"Hello. Can I get a cabana?"

"Are you staying in the hotel?" I glance down at "The Fontainebleau Hotel" stitched onto my robe, then look back up at the attendant.

"Yes?"

"Room number?"

"Nine-oh-one."

"How many people?"

"One."

"Yeah. We're all full."

It feels like we could have gotten to this quicker, but I don't want to go and sit in my room. Why would I relegate myself to where this whole business had begun—being sent to my room by forces other than personal choice? The guy stares blankly at me, then goes back to folding towels. I stand, not knowing the next move. A gravelly voice then calls out from a cabana directly in front of me.

"Hey Eric, *más agua, por favor.*"

"Sure thing, Señor Perez." Eric the cabana attendant takes off like a bullet. I stand there, peering into the dark of the cabana. After a moment a man steps out into the light, shading his eyes with his hand, squinting quizzically at me.

"*Hola, señorita,* are you lost?" This time I actually point at the insignia on my robe.

"No, I belong here." The man smiles.

"Where are your parents?"

"They're not here."

"Well, who are you with? You want me to get Eric to find them?"

"No, that's okay. I'm here by myself but I'm leaving for the airport in a few hours, so . . . it's okay." The man's smile starts to fade slightly; he then steps out farther into the sun.

"Wait, you're here alone, at the hotel?"

"Yes." He gives a dark look around at the pool deck.

"I do not think you should be here alone." Two grannies walk by in swimming caps that look like chrysanthemums.

"It is a very dangerous place," he adds. I couldn't really speak to this, but my whole experience of the past twenty-four hours has been so bizarre that arriving at a point where I was apparently in danger seemed plausible.

"Why?" I say. "What might happen?"

"People can be very bad," he says. This makes sense.

"Why don't you come and sit in here with my wife and me

and our friends and I will call up to the front desk and make sure they know where you are." It's very hot in my robe; my beak is slipping, and I really need a drink of water.

"Okay," I say, never for a moment thinking that this man could be one of the bad people about which he spoke.

The cabana is lovely. Señor Perez sits me down at the table and makes an announcement in Spanish to those already seated there. His wife, who is the only woman present, makes a tutting sound when he gets to what must have been the bit about me being alone. She pours me a glass of lemonade from the jug on the table and motions for me to take off my hat and sunglasses/beak. There is a pause in the conversation while they review my presence, then they all start chatting again in Spanish and I drink my lemonade. Señor Perez comes back to the table, having called up to the front desk from a courtesy phone and says,

"Yes. You are alone, they have told me. They asked if you were being any trouble. I told them no. Have you been causing trouble before?" I sit back against my chair and look Señor Perez directly in the eyes. *This is a man*, I think, *who deserves a straight answer.*

"Well, my dad thinks I caused trouble, but I don't think I did. I think it might have looked like trouble to him, but to me it was something else." Señor Perez looks thoughtfully at me and rests his elbows on the table and his chin on his interlaced hands.

"Hmm. I know something about this. Trouble can be very subjective. Do you know what subjective means?"

"No."

"It is how a person sees things. It is the way they themselves see things, not necessarily how others may see it."

This is fantastic news.

"Trouble *is* subjective," I say, "but then why can't other people know they are being subjective and that someone else might be being subjective too?"

"Oh, they can. But people don't like to think they are wrong. People *really* like to be right."

"But then how do you know who is *actually* right?" I say. Señor Perez smiles and shrugs.

"You don't."

I am perplexed by what seems to be an ongoing situation in life as a child: you identify something, an adult offers clarity on why it is that way, you feel relieved, but then after further interrogation of the *why*, the whole thing falls apart with the acknowledgment that to some questions there is no resolution.

"Where did you come from?" Señor Perez asks.

"Barbados." I sigh.

"I was sent away from an island too," he says. "They said I caused trouble."

"What did you do?"

"I disagreed with the government. To them, that was trouble."

"Why couldn't you just talk about it with them?" Señor Perez smiles broadly if not sadly at me, then looks up at the rest of the table and says something in Spanish to get their attention. He then gestures to me and clearly recounts the gist of what we had been saying. The table explodes into laughter. The men slap their hands on their legs and a few of them repeat,

"¡Hablar con ellos!" loudly, between laughs.

Señor Perez looks back at me and says kindly,

"Sometimes people *see* only the trouble, they don't want to talk about it." *That is exactly it*, I think. Sometimes they see only the trouble.

"So, do you know what made your father send you away?"

"Yes."

"You don't have to tell me what it was. It doesn't matter. What matters is that you know what you did, and you have to decide if you believe you were right. You may never know why someone else does what they do, but you can always know that about yourself. Know what you believe. Commit to it. It makes sometimes being punished for it easier to bear."

He has been taking little nips from a medium-size bottle with "Havana Gold" written on the side, and his wife gently leans over and removes the bottle from his hands and puts it in her purse without breaking conversation with the man sitting next to her. Señor Perez stares at his empty hands and then at me.

I realize a few things at once. First, I believe I was right to be angry with my father for aligning with his girlfriend's feelings over my own. I was less sure about why that was, and if it were a grown-up thing or a dad thing. I did know that clearly people don't like it when you vocally disagree with the choices they make, whether they are your dad or not. I was fairly sure I understood what Señor Perez was saying, though: choose which battles are worth fighting in the name of your own belief. I look around at the pool deck, this sequestered space full of people I didn't know, with a room upstairs full of stuff I didn't want, and I wonder if it is worth it, I wonder if my father had at any point in the last day and night, leaned against the doorjamb of my empty room and asked himself if it had been worth it too.

Señor Perez looks like he might also be thinking hard thoughts.

And there we sit. Two dissidents examining their paths to the same cabana. There wasn't a single answer to the question of exile, but there was the prudence of adding it in as a potential destination if you were troublemakers, like Señor Perez and me.

I stand up slowly and thank the table for having made room for me. Then I turn and tell Señor Perez I should probably go and pack, as I have rather a lot of extra luggage. I hold out my hand to shake but he hugs me instead and says,

"*Hermanita. Adios.*"

"*Adios,*" I say. Then I turn and set off across the concrete badlands, robe in hand, sunglasses and beak in place, face to the unforgiving sun.

3

BUTTERFLY HAIR

You have to understand my hair. To fully contextualize this story my hair requires your investment in it as a nonverbal but alarmingly expressive and independent character. It would do well in a Fellini movie. Even as I sit here now it is fighting the fact that it is rooted to my scalp and reaches out longingly, as if each spiraling strand heard there was somewhere much better to be in the north, south, east, and west.

When I was at school, along with being called 50p face (a 50p is a seven-sided British coin), I was also called Slash, Animal, and T. Rex; these refer (in order) to: Guns N' Roses, the Muppets, and Marc Bolan. These had not always been accurate reflections of my hair, however, and no one was more surprised than I was when, with the advent of boarding school—with no nanny or mum manning the hair dryer—my previously wavy, silky locks, left to air-dry with no further intervention, now doubled in size and appeared to reach up and out, away from my face, like giant springs pogoing in perpetual motion.

For me, the late '70s and early '80s are remembered not for the music or the clothes, not burgeoning Thatcherism, Reaganism, or indeed, Ayatollahism, but for the hair gel. It was thick, radioactive-green gel, and it came in a clear tub. I can't recall its name, but if you're old enough, it has to be the only one you too remember, because there wasn't anything else. It is a credit to modern-day product development that today I could make a realistic effigy of my entire family using only the hair product containers in my bathroom. My early deprivation has made me a greedy consumer of any product that tames my hair to a place where I look, at the very least, approachable.

Back in the day, that green gel had a simple protocol: first, if applied after a shower in the evening, it would solidify your hair to the density of concrete, then a fusing process would occur whereby one big dreadlock greeted you the next day. I was aware of the consequences of using the evil stuff, but with sweet naïveté and hope, I continued doing the same thing over and over again, expecting a different result. It was only much later that I found out this was actually a definition of insanity.

I soldiered on through weddings and parties; a soft-focus fuzz in the back of pictures, always smiling, always wishing I had a hat. I looked at some of those pictures the other day and saw again the gaping chasm that physically existed between me and my mother and my sister Kate; they were elongated blondes, graceful and contained, with huge smiles that were simultaneously warm and removed, they were sylph-like Ariels to my primal Caliban; as sleek and unbothered as I was messy and impassioned. They both had the straightest hair you could imagine.

In the summer of 1983, my mother's marriage to my stepfather was in its death throes. We had very little money, but in the close quarters of a tiny cottage in Hampshire, all any of us wanted to do was get away—anywhere—for some kind of vacation. A hotel was found in Arcachon, a seaside town in Bordeaux, and my mother, my sister, and I along with our five-year-old brother Ed set off to find respite from the emotional turmoil of rural England.

Our poor mother. Now, having experienced the kind of heartbreak that leaves your head resting gently against the bathroom floor, I understand the profound need to sometimes pull a geographical and run away from pain. It must have been very difficult that we all had to run away from pain with her.

We arrived in Arcachon, the middle of the night, to a hotel located on the third floor of a crumbling turn-of-the-century building. A Chinese restaurant occupied the first two floors, and the air smelled dramatically of kung pao croissants. We woke up the next morning to a roar of traffic and ninety-degree heat in the only French town I have ever known to be perky. We could all fit on the sliver of balcony if we stood in a horizontal line with our backs pressed against the outside wall, and from that vantage point we looked down with collective dread on all the bustling, chatty people in the street. Mum, determined to be bright and to mine the experience for something good, said everything was going to be fine and that we were going to find a lovely beach. Her voice was pitched way too high for us to believe the bit about everything being fine, but the beach sounded all right. In front of the tiny mirror in the bathroom, my sister and I looked at ourselves. She ran a hand through her long blond hair, sighed, and adjusted the waistband of her shorts.

"Get dressed, Minnow."

"I am dressed."

"That's the T-shirt you slept in."

"I know. But it covers everything up."

"We are not religious. You are clearly a loony."

I looked in the mirror, and her appraisal couldn't really be faulted. My T-shirt went to my knees and my hair was a crackling fizz, rebelling wildly at France and her maximum humidity. My hair already said far too much—I could reveal nothing further with my body.

On the beach, my T-shirt pulled over my knees, I sat looking at Kate. There, with tourists packed around her like racks of sunburned cutlets on a sandy grill, she looked dreamy, feline, and utterly perfect. At thirteen I genuinely believed if I could look like her everything would be better; that without my freckled curves and fright wig hair, the knot in my stomach would unfurl, the pitted road to popularity, boys, and the rest of my life would smooth into an open plain of charm and fortune. I knew so little of the inner workings of her mind and heart, that her exterior was truly all I focused on; it was also an excellent diversion from my own.

We ate lunch in an overpriced beach café. After one small bite, my brother offered his sweaty cheese sandwich to a cadaverous dog lurking nearby. I couldn't blame him, it was a drooping tourist sandwich concocted by a café that was clearly sick of pandering to the British:

"Can I get normal bread, not the long, stick stuff?" said the woman at the next table.

"Can I get mayonnaise with my Brie?" said her husband.

The dog, though hungry, maintained his Gallic pride and wouldn't touch the sandwich either.

"Well, what *do* you want to eat then, Eddie?" asked Mum.

"Strawberries."

"Okay, we'll get strawberries."

They came, they looked bad, he ate them anyway, and we headed back to our towels.

We sat back down in the searing heat and almost immediately Ed started to look green.

"Am going to throw up, Mummy."

"No, no, no, don't throw up, darling, those were very expensive, delicious strawberries and you loved them!"

"Am going to be sick, though."

My mother spoke with a strained, calm voice, as if to a gunman:

"Please don't."

He could not comply. I realized we had reached rock bottom far sooner than we usually did on family vacations. I watched Mum gently hold Ed over the water's edge, and with each retch, she counted out the net worth of the strawberries:

"Ten francs! Oh, darling, do stop . . . fifteen . . . twenty! They cost almost a hundred francs. You mustn't be sick anymore, hold on to the last eighty if you possibly can."

He looked at my mother as he threw up the last eighty francs of rotten strawberries, and presumably would have given a very French shrug had he not been five and British. We all reassembled on our towels, and Kate and I stared down the most vocally revolted of the surrounding beachgoers. I thought my mother was going to cry.

"Don't worry, Mum, Min and I have money Dad gave us, we'll spend that," said Kate.

"We'll do no such thing, that's your special money, come on, let's go and walk around town."

Mum jumped to her feet, fully done with this particular nightmare and apparently eager for the next.

"I quite fancy cutting off all my hair," said Kate, to no one in particular. "You know, like Siobhan from Bananarama."

"Well then, let's find a hairdresser!" said Mum, suddenly reinvigorated by the thought of an actual plan. I was stupefied.

"Why would you cut off all your hair? You have perfect hair . . . I mean, it's perfect."

"It's annoying," she said.

I was incensed. Annoying? Long, straight blond hair "annoying"? I imagined having so much perfection going on that I could actually be annoyed by some of it. We wandered along the seafront and there, between two bars, was a hair salon called La Jolie Fille. It looked fairly un*jolie*, but there was a smiling man waving through the window, so we went in. Inside was somewhere between a barbershop and a hair salon; the waving man seemed to be the only person about.

"*Bonjour,*" said Kate. "*Je voudrais couper mes cheveaux.*" (Hello, I would like to cut my hair.)

"*Ah bon, asseyez–vous, mademoiselle.*" (Great, sit yourself down, missy.)

Mum spoke perfect French and translated when Kate's schoolgirl version ran out. The man didn't know Siobhan from Bananarama, but he had trimmed Olivia Newton-John's hair in the late '70s so everyone felt we were pretty much good to go. I leaned against the sink and watched in fascinated horror as he tied her hair in a ponytail and then chopped it off. Her hair fell in a bobbed curtain around her cheekbones. He took an electric razor and shaved the nape of her neck, then cut the hair on the back of her head to about an inch till it sloped fantastically, all the way down to the longer pieces around her face. She looked staggering, and I felt tears burning at the back of my eyes. It wasn't the revelation that she could look even more beautiful—I had no doubt that her beauty would always evolve (even as I felt my own had barely made it to the equivalent of a single-celled organism)—it was the complete confidence with which she'd just changed herself, and now the easy way in which she got up from the chair, brushed her lap, and said,

"*Merci, monsieur.* Shall we go and get an ice cream, Mum?"

I gripped the sink. I wanted so much to be what I was not, and maybe in an empty hair salon, with just me and the hairdresser on the inside of my chrysalis, I wondered if my butterfly wings might be revealed. I couldn't wait for eclosion, and scissors suddenly seemed pertinent to emergence.

"I think I'd quite like a haircut too."

Mum and Kate looked at me.

"Okay, darling, but do remember last time . . ." Mum trailed off.

"Your hair's quite hard to, you know . . ." Kate trailed off.

"I know but I'd like to. Now. Really, you go and get an ice cream and I'll stay here."

"Well, all right," said my mother warily. "But don't let him take too much off. *Pas trop, monsieur, pas trop.*"

"*Bien, madame.*"

They left and I sat in the chair. The man and I looked at each other in the mirror.

"*Je voudrais la même chose que ma soeur, s'il vous plaît.*" (The same thing as my sister, please.)

He smiled and shrugged. "*Mais vous n'êtes pas votre soeur.*" (But you are not your sister.)

I said with a laugh, "*Evidement.*" (Obviously.) "*S'il vous plaît, monsieur*" (Please . . .)

He looked at me long and hard and checked the spring in my tangled puff of hair.

"*La vie est une bonne école. Porquoi-pas une coupe?*" (Life teaches us useful lessons. Why not a haircut?)

Except I didn't understand what he said.

He wet my hair down, ignored my mother's plea, and following the siren call that some hairdressers hear, he cut off all my hair. A long, graceful neck, one I hadn't had that morning, was revealed. Secret cheekbones appeared, defined by an ellipse of dark hair on either side. My moon face looked back at me from the mirror; I looked peaceful without the chaos of my curls; dark hair, slick across my head, looked so beautiful and new. I smiled.

"*Merci, merci, monsieur.*" He patted my shoulder with a sweet kind of resignation and said,

"*Vous devez attendre jusqu'a ce qui'l soit sec.*" (You must wait until it dries.)

I sat on the seawall across the street from the salon, waiting for Mum and Kate and Ed. I felt the strangest sensation, foreign and welcome, which was one of being happy to be seen. My neck felt naked and glorious. There was space around my head; nature abhors a vacuum and surely something good would be sucked into that space I had determinedly created. I swung my legs up over the wall and crossed the road to wait under the salon's awning, as it was meltingly hot. Catching sight of myself in the window, I saw my big white T-shirt, my Minnie Mouse beach bag, and this strange helmet I hadn't previously been wearing. It took me a second to calibrate to the reflection, thinking for a moment it must be some distortion in the glass, and then with all the misery a thirteen-year-old duckling/caterpillar can harbor, I wailed quite loudly.

The hairdresser came and got me off the sidewalk. He sat me back in the chair, and my true reflection in the mirror galvanized my hysteria. Where had my sleek, Clara Bow butterfly gone? How could the tight, frizzy nonsense up around my ears now be my hair? How could bad hair be worse, and how could devolution happen so fast? Back inside the chrysalis, the hairdresser looked at me in the mirror.

"Vous êtes belle." (You are beautiful.)

This made me cry even harder, as he couldn't quite reach the cadence of conviction. He seemed caught between sadness and happiness.

"D'accord, d'accord, vous serez belle, de votre propre manière, un jour prochain." (All right, all right, you will be beautiful, in your own way, one day soon.) I took the scarf he handed me and tied it like a fortune teller. Mum and Kate and Ed walked back into the salon and stood behind the chair. Kate patted my scarfed head,

"That good, is it?"

"Oh, darling," said Mum, "do you want me to yell at him?"

"No. It's okay. He was only trying to help. You just can't help my hair, though."

"I like your face," said Ed.

The hairdresser said something to Mum that must have

amounted to "I'm not gonna charge you and keep the scarf."
Then he leaned down to me and said,

"*Ma petite, vous n'êtes pas tes cheveaux.*" (Sweetheart, you are
not your hair.)

He was wrong, though, because I was. My hair was just
part of my identity that had shown up too soon for the rest of
me to accommodate. I had banished it for a while, but it would
be waiting for me in the future, when perhaps I'd have the
tools, both literally and emotionally, to embrace it.

4

OTHER PEOPLE'S DRUGS

It was late spring, and I was graduating from drama school, having been robustly instructed by every teacher in every department that unemployment was assured. There was a cheerful parsing of this information. We were kids. We were hubris personified. "Unemployment" seemed like one of those words adults used to frighten us into modifying our youth. Presumably to accommodate their failure.

I'd always been interested in the acting teachers I'd had. Their passionate rigor in sharing the fundamental disciplines of acting. Their highlighting the pitfalls and traps apparently set for me personally, by Shakespeare. The importance they placed on square shoulders and a deeply supported voice. All of these lessons were imparted in a slightly masonic way, as though I were being let in on profound secrets. All the teachers believed acting could not actually happen correctly unless you followed certain intractable rules. I have no idea if they were right. To this day, I have no idea if I am acting correctly. I do know I often refer back to the commitment of those teachers' beliefs, though. They really, really believed in the framework they were selling.

I wonder if, when teaching something as ephemeral as acting, you have to do this, and that building a scaffold around a muse is how you tether yourself to her. It's only now, looking back, that I realize how much of what they taught was mulled with this secret knowledge, only relayed in the last moments of their teaching: That for all your adherence to discipline, your observance of the rules of iambic pentameter and how to sit down while wearing a sword without crushing your balls—the chances of you making a living as an actor are cadaverously slim.

Trying to skew the odds in your favor is a huge part of your job in the months leading up to graduation. You write sackloads of letters to talent agencies and casting directors imploring them to come and see you in one of your final shows. The most passionate letters are reserved for when you are playing a proper, juvenile leading role and not the granny. Although I played many memorable grannies, according to my mother. They were not memorable in the "What a sublime transformation, I can't believe the actor is only nineteen" way, but rather "Who is that face-pulling hunchback in the back with the three lines and the earhorn?"

My big role had been in Tennessee Williams's *Camino Real*, playing Marguerite "Camille" Gautier. This in itself had been slightly problematic. Camille is an aging, consumptive courtesan. I'd definitely love to sink my teeth into that role right about now in my life, but in my late teens it was an astonishing stretch to believe I was anything other than robustly bouncy in both appearance and spirit. I do not believe a nineteen-year-old can disappear into the role of an aging anything, particularly that of a disappointed middle-aged woman with tuberculosis. I had a go at the cough, though.

"Goodness, of all the Tennessee Williams plays to put on, they picked *that* one?" queried my mother. "*Not* his finest. And essentially about dealing with getting old and becoming irrelevant. What on *earth* would you know about that?"

"Not much" was the answer.

"I thought you were supposed to have at least one part where you got to play a young person. What happened?"

"I think they ran out."

While my letters of entreaty to the agents and casting directors had been met with the polite agreements of attendance, the anticipated feedback, postshow, had in fact turned out to be a resounding silence.

And so it was that the final performance in my collegiate life happened, in a black box studio space, above a pub in Southwest London. By the last echo of applause, that weakly met my last performance, I had uncharacteristically rather given up. Every single person in my small class of sixteen had gained some sort of theatrical representation in our final year. I had not, and I was not furnished with any plan for life beyond this moment. I definitely intended to rally, but not right now. In this moment I settled into the bleakness of my prospects.

The good thing about doing a play in a pub is that you're in a pub. When all is said and done, there is only the smallest distance between your disappointment/triumph and the bar. There we stood, a packet of salt and vinegar crisps, and me and my mother. The two free glasses per family of warm white wine were going down fast. Castmates shuffled about with their parents and their spiffily dressed reps. It was a hollow feeling, staring back along the pathway I had cut with my desire to be an actress. Its shape a fairly straight line, no twists as yet, due to the shortness of my life experience. And here I was, my desire intact but all the practical actions I'd taken to manifest it apparently used up. I had come to a premature full stop.

"I am the only person here who doesn't have an agent," I said, with convincing drama.

"Nonsense," said Mum, who was inured to convincing self-pity. "I don't have one either." She laughed. I did not laugh.

"Come on. Let's go home," she said.

We swigged the last of the wine and finished off the crisps. A matter-of-fact Eucharist, genuinely feeling like the Last Supper.

The next morning, I woke up in mental free fall. The end of the road had become a very tall building from which I was now falling. Crashing backward down through every play, musical, and dance class, through the required reading lists set by so many ingenious teachers, through the home-made costumes, and every empty sky with one, lone star that

I had fervently wished upon. I saw the nights where I was in the audience at the theater, refusing to sit back against my seat but rather balancing on its edge, wishing I could claw my way to the stage and enter the drama unnoticed . . . but then be noticed.

The mountain of focused experiences that I had been clumsily climbing my whole life (to what I thought was a happy and inevitable peak) lay around me in rubble. I suddenly realized that circumstances are not weight-bearing. They do not create a structure upon which to safely build your life. Circumstances can change in an instant. And that shifting can stop plans from manifesting. My plan was now just an idea that apparently had run its course.

So what was I supposed to do now that I'd done everything I thought I was supposed to do?

There was only one man to ask.

"Dad. It's all gone tits up. Current coordinates: failure to launch. Prospects undetermined. I don't even know what I'm supposed to want."

Dad sat in his tiny front garden in London with the expansiveness of a man on vacation in the Dordogne.

"Ah. Well. You gotta write a list with the headers: existential and practical. What you want is written in both those columns. You want to pay your rent. You want to eat. You want to make real your dream of working as an actress. You want to be rich and famous."

"I don't really want that. I just want Richard Ayre to notice me and think I'd make a brilliant Lady Macbeth."

"Too specific," said Dad. "You gotta keep the intention clear but stay out of how it manifests."

"This feels like you're asking me to be way more evolved than I actually am," I countered.

"Gotta aim high, darling. And sometimes taking your eye off the ball and focusing on more practical stuff is how you get the ball in the back of the net."

There were a lot of metaphors going on and, I think, partial distillation of a few self-help books I'd given him. I tried to translate:

"So . . . figure out what I need to do practically, identify what my dreams are, then forget about the dreams and make them come true by doing the practical shit?"

"That, my darling, is the gist of my sermon, yes." He turned his face to the sun, which had momentarily appeared from behind the permaclouds.

"I can also give you fifty pounds." I kissed the top of his head.

"Thanks, Dad."

That night I had a gig at Blushes, a restaurant whose coy name belied the amount of drugs being done in the bathroom. We were a small combo: piano, upright bass, and drums. That night I wanted to do a lot of sad Nancy Wilson: "The Masquerade Is Over" and "Face It Girl, It's Over." When the band tried to persuade me into some happier fare I doubled down and launched into "Everything Happens to Me." I started singing before the band was ready and so began in an awkward a cappella. By the time I got to "I guess I'll go through life just catching colds and missing trains" the bass player was rolling his eyes. We finished up. The band was annoyed. Emotion is great when channeled into performance; however, wayward self-pity can come across as a bit indulgent and unfortunately that's where I'd been operating from all evening.

"Cheer it up a bit next time, would you?" brayed Stuart, the restaurant's manager, as we departed. "People want jolly music while they're eating their dinner."

"Eating their dinner? I think you mean doing lines off the back of the toilet tank," said Mike, the drummer. "But sure, we'll cheer it up for you next time, and you might want to wipe your nose." Stuart's right nostril was rimmed like a salted margarita glass.

I leaned against the door of the van while Mike loaded his drums.

"You can't inflict your shit on an audience. They're there to be entertained," he said.

"But I thought you said they were all just in the back doing drugs."

"Yeah, I mean they were. But it's a bad habit to get into."

"What, drugs?"

"No, getting lost in whatever you're personally going through at the expense of your performance. Use it, don't telegraph it." He looked a bit weary. He had toured with Sinéad O'Connor and I understood that he was now playing joints that largely acted as waiting rooms till the clubs opened. If people were disinterested in eating in these restaurants we'd been playing, they were even less interested in listening to the background music. We were both definitely not living our dream.

"Does it bum you out playing places like this?" I asked.

"Yeah, but I've got kids now, any work is good." His wife had just had twin girls.

"Anyway, cheer up, Sinéad," he said. "That's what I used to say to Sinéad."

I laughed. This was a joke he made quite often.

"What did you call the twins again?" I said. He grinned, hoisting his snare case into the van and closing the doors, then going along with our newest joke:

"Anna one Anna two."

I called my friend Isla. She had been a child actor on a really successful sitcom and now lived off the residual checks. We were both the same age, but she had definitely already lived some of her dreams in my estimation. I'm not sure what her ambitions were beyond having a really good time, but she radiated positivity and was always incredibly sunny about the worst situations:

"I'm being evicted. It's great—I'll have to get rid of all this stuff I never use!"

"I totaled my car, but because it's completely written off, the insurance is gonna pay the full whack!"

I told her a bit about the current free fall and asked her what she did when she had absolutely no idea what to do.

"Ooo shit, just let me skin up, that question is really heavy."

I heard her rustling for rolling papers and casting around for a cigarette to dissect.

"God, I really hope this is actual hash," she said. "The last time I bought any off that idiot Bill the Bong, it was an eighth of liquorice." Eventually I heard her spark up and she spoke as she inhaled deeply.

"Right, right, what do I do when I don't have a plan, ummm . . ." she exhaled with a satisfied sigh.

"Well, I just do this really. Get high and see what happens."

This made total sense. For her. I'd smoked a lot of weed and hash previously when I was a student with a giant plan, because blurring the edges when you're not worried felt fine. My plan was my safety net. The gently swinging hammock supporting my stoned state, making it temporal and not a place I had to stay to feel safe. Now the idea of being high and unable to feel the urgent, keen edges of an uncharted future felt insane.

Isla purred into the phone.

"I think the first thing you gotta do when you're really feeling the oblivion is amplify the oblivion. Make friends with it. Dance with it. Really fucking *get on one* with it. Buzzy said there's a rave this weekend up the A40. We should go. We should get into it."

"What's the 'A40'? Is it a club?"

"No, sis, it's actually up the A40 freeway, somewhere before Oxford, in a field."

House music had, by this time, made its way out of the warehouses of Chicago and beaten down the door of every club, car, house, and apparently field in England. Acid House was its cousin. The speedy, bloodshot vamp who didn't go to bed after a punishing all-nighter but instead stayed up, deifying the Roland TB-303 synthesizer and putting it squarely at the center of every track then created. The repetitions, solid beats, and never-ending lengths of tracks meant that if it was oblivion you were looking for, all forms of this new electronic dance music would happily serve as its soundtrack. Loop upon loop, sample upon sample, wave upon wave.

The following Saturday, at about 10:30 p.m., ten cars converged at a meeting point outside a pub in West London. One of the drivers knew where we were going, and off we set in convoy for the secret field in Oxfordshire.

My car was packed with randoms—and Isla, who was changing clothes in the passenger seat. There was a friend of

Isla's sister who had recently gotten out of prison; he missed the beginning of rave culture and was eager to catch up. And his girlfriend, who let us know she was a journalist for *The Guardian* but would not be writing about this experience. She was about sixteen times more threatening than her ex-con boyfriend. She kept telling me to "floor it" and I kept telling her, "Look, my car is a Ford Fiesta and built only for light grocery shopping." She sneered and called me fucking middle-classed.

Truth as invective has always puzzled me. Later, when I had been shot out of the cannon into fame, I would see that it is a trope returned to by journalist after journalist. It has a strange queasy effect, reading something about yourself that is absolutely true but is presented as a fault: "She is tall and thin and eats very little for lunch." "Her teeth are always bared when she smiles." "None of her relationships has lasted more than a year."

I often wondered why they use truth as an assault when there were more devastating weapons available. Before social media offered a platform to do so, I wanted so many times to rejoin:

"Don't you realize how unimaginative and toothless it is to call me what I am? You'd really do far more damage sneering at me for what I'm not—for all the things I have tried so hard to be and have so far failed at. Honestly, ask me like, three questions about myself and I'll give you proper ammo for a more interesting assassination."

"Don't mind her," said the journalist's boyfriend. "She doesn't have a car and I was banged up for stealing one. Cars set her off."

The guy stuffed in the backseat, next to these two, started laughing. He was clearly very tall, as his legs were pulled up to his chin and his head scraped the top of the Fiesta at a funny angle. I'd been looking at a road map while my car filled up with people and hadn't noticed him before.

"Perhaps she'd like to walk," he said, "as 'cars set her off'?"

"I just want to get there before it turns into a total scrum," said the journalist, whose name was Harriet.

"I think you might be disappointed to learn that 'scrum' is by definition what a rave is and if you're looking for something a bit more genteel then you're probably gonna want to fuck off back to Chelsea, love."

I looked at the tall man through the rearview mirror—newly heroic and cheerfully crushed into my tiny car—and I knew that I loved him. Hot on the heels of this realization was the accompanying acknowledgment that it did not take a great deal for me to fall in love. Being defended, considerateness, a train door held open, making room on a crowded pub bench—these things regularly not only triggered my devotion, they also were watertight assurances of my lifelong happiness with this new stranger. The thing was, I was completely aware of how nuts it was to feel a whole life together on the back of a kind word, but it never stopped me from falling in love.

As a truly terrible person I once fell in love with said when I told him I first loved him after he'd given me a lift home:

"That's not just nuts, it's also crazy."

We arrived in the designated field. Two hundred cars were parked haphazardly, and you could feel the bass thumping up from the ground, through our feet, and whatever crops we were destroying. The music was coming from a huge corrugated iron barn some ways off. We got out of the car and stood staring at the barn through the gloom. The tall guy really was immense—six-foot-six, conservatively.

"God, you're enormous," I blurted.

"And you're not fat!" he blurted back. "I genuinely thought you were!"

"I know, "I said, "it's my face. I got mad cheeks."

"You *do*," he said with a smile. "And it really makes no difference to me if you're fat or not but the difference between sitting-down-you and standing-up-you offers a proper optical illusion."

"Are you high?" I asked.

"Not as high as I'm going to be in about half an hour." And with that he took off across the field.

Harriet and the car thief were also already jogging awkwardly toward the music.

"Meet back here at 6:00 a.m.!" I shouted.

"Fuck 'em," said Isla.

She stood next to me like a warrior about to go into battle. She had changed into an outfit of raveworthy confection, Day-Glo bike shorts with a hot pink bikini over them, glow sticks stacked around her wrists and neck. She looked like she'd gotten dressed from a vending machine.

She snapped the lime green bum bag around her hips, checking off its contents.

"Right. Water, ChapStick, Band-Aids, chewing gum, drugs. Let's hustle, cupcake, Pete Tong's on at midnight"

I fell into step beside her and like the good party sergeant major she was, she halted right before we entered the fray and said,

"Okay. If we lose each other, don't worry. Don't forget to drink water. Meet back at the car at 6:00 a.m. Remember that the car is parked by the only tractor in the field. If the tractor is gone because the farmer is up early farming, look for the space where it used to be. Do not do more drugs than I give you, copy that?" She held out two pills with smiley faces imprinted on them.

"Ten-four. I'm not really going to be doing any drugs, though," I said.

"But what about oblivion?" She looked worried.

"Oh, don't worry, I'm literally at its gates. Definitely don't need any help getting in."

My proximity to nothingness seemed to mollify her.

"Well, that's your prerogative, cupcake, but good luck surviving in there without being off your fucking tits."

I genuinely didn't need the drugs. Most people, looking to "not feel" the panoply of their emotions, can find some activity, distraction, or synthetic high and avoid them for however long is sustainable. I've always found it impossible to suppress emotion, which can be exhausting, messy, and empowering in unequal measure, depending on your perspective. For me, drugs amplified whatever problem I was taking the drugs to get away from. I had taken enough of them in my short life to realize this. I had found, in the absence of having an alt helper to quell the constant churning of worry in my stomach, that the best thing to do was dance. And if I were to launch into the farthest reaches of my own personal oblivion, then I would do so fully compos mentis, at 130 beats per minute.

Dancing at a rave is bananas, and it's a particular gestalt—the whole being greater than the sum of its parts. The "parts" that night were all in different stages of ecstasy (the drug, not the emotion). Some sweat-slicked in closed-eyed heaven, some near to throwing up but breathing through it, some just grimly riding the wave of the four-to-the-floor beat, as if there were an actual destination to be reached.

I worked my way to the middle of the organism, raised

my hands in the air, and turned to face our night god, the DJ. He looked down beatifically on his tribe and while clutching a headphone to his right ear, tried to disentangle himself from a girl who'd jumped on his back and was licking the left one. I danced for hours. I did what the music said, followed where it led, and I felt my old plans slough off and get trampled underfoot. I mentally added coming back and dancing every weekend to the practical column of my list. I would stay awake in the heat and the dark of each appointed field or barn, I would let physical exhaustion empty me out and make space for some new map to be unfurled. Buoyed by my new nonplan plan, I saw that it was close to 6:00 a.m. and started to shuffle myself sideways through the throng. The tall guy from my car appeared on the other side of the crowd; he was waving his hands slowly in the air like a giant palm tree. I waved slowly back at him and tapped my watch to show him it was time to go. He gave me a big thumbs-up and carried on swaying. I managed to push my way to him and yelled,

"We gotta go!"

Saucer-eyed and content, he said, "I'm not leaving, it's lovely here."

"I promise you it's not," I said. "How will you get home?"

"Don't worry, my mum's here. She'll take me."

"Oh, I don't think she is, I think you're just really high," I said.

"Yeah, I am, but also she's the DJ." I looked up to the podium and saw that a woman in her forties had taken over and was now spinning slower grooves through the graveyard shift.

"Oh. Cool," I said. Well, see you around, Isla's got my number, you should call me." I started to push back out into the crowd, and he called out,

"Yeah, probably not, but see you around you sweet, big old moon face!"

I was glad our love affair had ended neatly.

Emerging out into the new day, I was greeted with the pastoral sight of a hundred party people changing their clothes out of the backs of their cars. The bass was still thumping from inside the barn, and birdsong from the fields sounded like reproach.

Arriving back at the car, Isla was dewy with her high and standing naked, arms stretched out, welcoming the sunrise.

"You came back," she breathed.

"Yes, of course I did."

"Not you. THE SUN." I tried not to roll my eyes at people on ecstasy, but it was quite hard. From the back of the car I handed her the pajamas she'd brought to change into and surveyed the mound of casualties heaped up against the passenger door.

"Isla, these are not the same people we came with." She looked vaguely at the people pile and said,

"Oh. yeah, these are people I made friends with. They all need a ride."

A girl leaning on the hood of my car and smoking a cigarette said,

"I'd be so grateful if you'd give them and me a ride back. I'm in charge of them. They have all recently thrown up, so please don't worry about the inside of your car." I appreciated the debriefing.

"Okay, well, get them inside, gimme a fiver for gas, and we're good to go."

She was small and pristine-looking for a raver. With the strength of a longshoreman, she hoisted each of her friends and stacked them in the backseat like sacks of grain. Isla had climbed in the trunk and was fast asleep.

"I'm Annie," she said, getting into the car. "Are you okay to drive?"

"Oh, yes," I said.

"You didn't do any e?"

"Nah. I'm high on life," I said rather grimly. She laughed.

"How could we go there and dance around in all that muck getting licked by strangers and not be out of it?"

I didn't tell her about wanting to remain conscious in oblivion; she might not have believed I wasn't on drugs.

"I just like to dance," she said, rolling down the window and propping her feet against the mirror. "And that sound system was banging."

"I like to dance too," I said. "In fact, I love it. Why do you think the expectation is to dance with someone else? I danced by myself for six hours straight and it was just so nice not to have to interact with anyone."

"I dunno," she said. "It's a weird social contract, like flailing around and expressing yourself is okay if you're both doing it but if you're doing it alone, you're a saddo who no one wants to dance with."

"Well, that is me for sure, and I wouldn't have it any other way," I said, wondering if this was in fact true. I stared at the empty freeway and thought about always wanting to be part of a collective but then somehow always managing to exile myself from it.

"Maybe it's tribal," I wondered aloud. "People do things in the safety of a group. Doing stuff by yourself, away from the herd, probably sends some primal message that you're diseased and close to death. Then it's shun city." She laughed at my gloom.

"All right, Eeyore, I think you might want to start looking at yourself as an independent woman who just doesn't want to be saddled with some sweat box grinding up on her all night."

"Yes," I said, "that is a better image than 'diseased outlier.'"

The Sunday sun gently turned my car into an oven, and the lumpen crew in the backseat began to groan as we pulled into Golden Square in Soho. Annie deftly hauled them all out of the car and stacked them on the curb.

"See you next week then?" she said, stretching like a cat while looking for a cab.

"Yeah. Isla said Dave Dorrell is playing at something in Acton. What's your phone number?"

She reached into her bum bag and got out a pencil and a piece of paper.

"Jesus. You and Isla have the world in your bum bags."

She laughed. "Yeah. Mary fucking Poppins, innit?"

I lay on my bed back at home, tired and awake. Plans, what plans? Those that I had were conceived in childhood and meant to be executed in adulthood. And here I was.

Intact and ready, the rough crayon drawing of life needed to become animated. I wanted to end up living in the square house with the curling smoke coming from the chimney, and on occasion to step into the princess dresses and sparkly heels. I was still the limitless drawing imagined by six-year-old me. I did not want her to be anything different, but I did need her to evolve.

The place I found myself stuck, at twenty, was being a new adult—still furnished with a child's dream plan, but being asked to manifest it in a world of adult expectations. It's a strange hallway that runs from the end of childhood to functioning adult. As someone who pretends for a living, this was its nascent point.

It's really sort of unbelievable that anyone lets you do it at all; like, when I had passed my driving test and took the "student driver" sign off the car to drive home from the testing center. I had still only driven a car by myself about fifteen times but there I was, careening through traffic in West London, everyone assuming I knew what I was doing. We all pretend until the pretense becomes practiced and, I suppose, looks like reality.

I carried on pretending to be a singer each night in a different club or restaurant. Jazz is the ultimate line drawing, leaving space for you to fill in and make it up. We'd take it in turns to play or sing over the instrumental section of "Let's Get Lost" as we were missing a trumpet to solo. When I was up, I'd play around with vocal improvs that either found a path or wound up in a ditch. Either way, it didn't matter, no one was listening, and I was free to pretend, garnering only pissed-off stares from the rest of the band when I'd truly (musically) thrown us all off the cliff.

On the weekends I'd show up in the designated meeting place, Isla would fill my car with our friends or with strangers, and we would set off for the secret rave location that by now everybody actually knew about. Each Saturday night I would meet the mental free fall I'd avoided all week and have a dance-off with it until one of us gave in.

Annie was always there at the end of the night. We never arrived together or met up in the middle of the action, we never saw each other midweek in town for a coffee and a chat, but we'd always find our way to the hood of my car as the sun came up on another Sunday morning and debate the brilliance of Sean Oliver and Neneh Cherry, who'd both been in a postpunk kind of jazzish band we loved called Rip Rig and Panic. Even though we were fueled by interest, by youth, and by unbridled enthusiasm, we'd sit like grannies, sipping tea out of the Thermos I'd brought, extremely smug in our sobriety as we watched people stagger around trying to find their cars.

It was late in the summer now; I could feel the specter of September waiting patiently to drag everyone back to school or to work. Back to life, back to reality. The threat felt real and urgent; September was bench pressing in the parking lot, biding its time until the calendar clicked over, at which point it would gently rest the weights on the rack and walk toward me saying, "Your ass is mine."

We were driving back from a party in Kings Cross on the last weekend in August. I'd shed so much weight over the summer from my strict diet of dancing and worrying, I'd bought the outfit I was wearing from a store for kids on The Kings Road.

"Dude, you're way too skinny," mused Annie, checking the label in the back of my T-shirt and seeing it was for a twelve-year-old. "You need a burger and an early night and a bucket of hair conditioner."

"Yes," I said, "the hair is out of control and I genuinely miss my ass."

"Are you a model?" she ventured.

"A MODEL?!" I screamed; I had always wanted someone to think I was a model. "YOU THINK I'M BEAUTIFUL??"

"Steady on," she replied. "I didn't mean a *model* model, I meant one of those tall, thin ones who look sort of arresting and a bit weird on the back of *i-D* magazine. Yeah, you're kind of cool-looking, but no offense, not *beautiful* like a Linda or a Christie or a Naomi."

"I don't care what kind you mean," I said, beaming, "you said 'model' and that's what I heard."

I realized through this whole summer we had never discussed what we did—if we had jobs, what our ambitions were. There had been so much music to discuss, so many books and places we wanted to travel to, so many boys we wanted to torture and also make out with.

"Well, I'm not a model. I sing, I play music, and I waitress when I have to. I'm supposed to be an actress."

"What do you mean 'supposed to be'?"

"I left drama school in April. No acting per se since then, so can't really say I *am* one."

"Did you get an agent?"

"No. I really thought I'd get one. I didn't have a plan if I didn't. I go to all these parties in lieu of a plan, but it's getting significantly harder to sustain this, knowing that I'm just avoiding the actual reality."

I'd come to a stop in a square in Soho, and she turned sideways to face me.

"Are you any good?"

"Well, I think so. It's quite hard to tell."

"Yeah, actors sort of need other people's agreement that they're good to really have proof *and* to get a job."

"God, it's depressing. It's so codependent before you're even out of the gate," I sighed.

"What do *you* do?" I then asked.

"I actually work for a casting director," she said, then quickly added, "Don't ask me if you can come in and meet her."

I stayed silent. I definitely would have asked that. I would have grasped the slender moment of serendipity with a viselike grip. I would never again have questioned the possibility of things turning around. I would have believed in magic. But as it was, pride and lack of negotiating skills kept me mute. I was horribly comfortable with my own impotence.

She burst out laughing,

"Oh, my God, you've gone bright red. I'm only fucking with you, of course you should come in and meet my boss. She'd love you."

It was the first Monday in September. I was on my way to Annie's office, which was actually the office of one of the great British casting directors, Leo Davis.

At drama school an acting teacher very specifically, perhaps too specifically, told us: "Always wear a hat when meeting casting directors—they are more likely to remember you." That morning, getting dressed, I'd struggled to reconcile this advice with my hair. As I looked in the mirror, I felt, on one hand, that a hat would contain my hair, and would also check the "memorable" box (assuming the casting director's office is questionnaire-centric).

On the other hand, I thought, my hair is already *like* a hat, therefore was wearing one a good idea if ultimately it looked like I was wearing two by mistake? Would this force the addition of a new box and would that one be labeled "more memorable" or "idiot"?

I opted for no hat, and as I walked down Portobello Road, felt myself hair-reaching for Jennifer Beals or Sigourney Weaver, knowing I'd probably have to settle for Slash. I didn't know exactly what Leo Davis could do for me. I mean, I knew she could cast me in a film, but that seemed unlikely right off the bat, and if Annie had told her how we had met, Leo Davis would surely think I was just some chancer who had nothing better to do than not take drugs at raves, in fields, in the Cotswolds.

I was sweating through what I'd hoped would remind Leo Davis of a Robert Palmer backup dancer's dress. My tights had laddered, and the autumn wind had increased my hair to Slash squared.

The office was in a basement next door to a record shop called Rough Trade. As I descended the wrought iron stairs, Bomb the Bass was thumping through the wall and I squeezed past two girls heading up, both wearing hats and clutching résumés.

Annie was out running an errand. Leo greeted me with the warmest smile.

"Are you Minnie?"

"Yes, Minnie Driver. I could probably make up another name if you think it'd be better."

"Well, it already sounds made up, so I wouldn't worry." She laughed and gave me a cup of tea. "Annie says you're funny and that you've read a lot of books."

"Yes, I have a list a teacher gave me. I'm working my way through it."

"What's next on the list?"

"The Fountainhead."

"Ooooo, fuck that—use it as a door stopper."

I loved Leo Davis.

"Okay," she said, "I've got ten minutes. Tell me your life story."

"Oh, it might take a bit longer than that."

"How old are you?"

"Twenty."

"It really shouldn't take longer than that."

I launched into the stories of school and Barbados, of music and plays written and performed to no one, or someone, if they were there. I told her about my plan and how big and certain it felt until it didn't. I beat the ten-minute timer by about thirty seconds and then sat there saying nothing, feeling lighter for the confession.

"Well," said Leo, "that's a good story." She looked at me thoughtfully. "I'm going to call someone for you. Let's see what they say."

She picked up the phone, dialed, and launched into a whole conversation about an actor I'd never heard of with the person who'd picked up. I could hear the other person's voice fairly clearly through the receiver of the big old telephone. Eventually Leo said,

"I've got someone here I think you should meet."

"Oh, yes?" said the voice. "Who's that?"

"She's called Minnie, she went to Webber Douglas."

"Oh, God, she has sent me literally a hundred letters about representation. Megan went to see her in a show. Wasn't great, don't think she's for us."

"Really? I think she's funny," said Leo. Why don't you let me send her over for a cup of tea." I'd had three cups already. I would happily drink a lot more. Tea seemed to be key in the new plan that was formulating. There was silence and then a sigh at the other end of the phone.

"Okay, send her over, but tell her she's only got ten minutes."

"I already did. Thank you, Lou." She hung up and looked at me, "You got all that then?"

"Yes," I said. "Ten minutes, be funny."

"Exactly," said Leo. "Good plan."

5

SETTLING DUST AND
THE SOUND OF CRICKETS

The apartment I lived in above my dad's garage was 520 square feet. Newly returned from Ireland after eight weeks of shooting my first movie, *Circle of Friends*, I sat on the small sofa and stared at my huge suitcases. There were so many of them. What had I packed for—a roaring social life after filming for twelve hours a day in a small village in southeastern Ireland? The village did have a diverse ratio of postwork activities, with nine pubs, two churches, and a grocery store (that was also the post office), but that shop closed at 4:00 p.m.

I *had* purchased quite a lot of sweaters. Everybody's auntie or granny or hard-up friend ("Sure he left her with the four children after robbing all their piggy banks and moving in with some floozy, bogtrotter from Clonown") knitted sweaters for cash. They saw me coming: chapped lips, chilly, purple knuckles, and a sizable bosom that they might have seen as their spiritual duty to help conceal. Their sweaters kept me nice for God.

I'm not sure what I had expected upon my return. Phones ringing off the hook, I suppose, thick ivory cards on top of my nonexistent fireplace inviting me to parties in Cannes. Barely having time to unpack all my Aran sweaters before heading off to do another movie with a handsome, floppy-haired actor like Hugh Grant, if not the actual Hugh Grant.

One leading role in a movie and I thought the shape of life would suddenly look different. How could all of that excitement, all of that adventure and creativity not have conga-lined its way off the set and into my real life. *Jesus,* I thought, *wanting to do this job is insane.*

You don't just have to win the lottery, you have to keep winning it again and again and again, and who the fuck is going to have that much luck?

The ten grand I'd been paid for *Circle of Friends* had seen off the mountainous debt I'd accrued. It also bought four new tires for the Ford Fiesta, which at this point was more piñata than party: the aftermath of a Fiesta, a mechanical hangover on wheels. I'd loaned the car to Isla while I'd been gone, and I think she might have actually lived in it and thrown some memorable parties.

The suitcases loomed like relics, monuments of a recent past, their semicircle giving off serious Druid vibes, reminding me I was in need of a soothsayer.

I called my agent.

"Ah, you're back," she said cheerfully. "Great. I expect you'd like a nice rest."

"No, not really. I'd quite like another job, actually."

"Ah, yes. Well, I'll definitely call you if anything like that comes up."

"Is there anything on the horizon?"

"Oh well, there's always something on the horizon—though who knows how close it will actually get."

"Well, you will presumably?"

"Yes, fingers crossed."

We hung up. I thought that if the soothsayer in my life was crossing fingers and that I was a lottery winner who needed to win again, then I should probably just tuck in, here on my Easter Island sofa with my Moai suitcases and wait for the future to happen.

The phone rang.

"Ah!" It was my agent again. "You must have magical powers."

I looked at my suitcases.

"They want to see you for a commercial tomorrow, don't think it's a very *good* commercial and hardly any money even if you did get it, but it's an audition, and you're great at those, so onward and upward. I'll call you back with the address."

My suitcases shrugged their luggage tags as she hung up—an audition is not a job and a commercial is not a film, but hey!

"There are no small parts, only small actors," said some-one brilliant like Maggie Smith or Stanislavsky. "I *am* good at auditions," I said triumphantly, standing up from the sofa. "I shall go to that audition and I shall get that shitty job!"

I called Isla. "We are going to the pub to celebrate!"

"Oooo, what are we celebrating?"

"Mediocrity, but on a grand scale."

"I will dress appropriately," she said solemnly.

Two days later I hurried down Brewer Street in Soho, found the casting office for the audition, and signed my name on the clipboard in the anteroom. The room was already filled with girls. There's a strange feeling when you walk into a casting call full of actresses, everyone's nice, but it's slightly serrated.

Each girl was in her best pick-me! outfit but there were a few subcategories of approach in general. Some had already given up, having noted that the girl sitting next to them had gotten the last three jobs they had both gone up for. Some appeared to be completely disinterested in the whole process and indicated that they had much loftier things to be get-ting on with: another script that they must busily highlight, a loud inquiry to the casting assistant about how long this might take as there were four more auditions to get to that morning. The smiley chatterbox who asked you where you'd bought every single thing you were wearing and interspersed each question with an "I'm never gonna get this." The steel in her eyes, though, said she actually thought she might.

Eventually my name was called, and I was ushered into a large room with more people in it than I had expected. Usually at a casting, it's the casting director, an assistant operating the camera, and sometimes the director. This room was filled with almost two rows of chairs in a wide semicircle, every seat taken by a man in a suit, mostly with their jackets over the back of the chair and their ties loosened. A stool stood in front of the semicircle and next to it was a tall receptacle, like you see next to the sofas in a hotel lobby, you know, an ashtray, but it was filled with pieces of chocolate.

"Okay, lovey," said the bored director, "pop your coat off and just leave it on the floor as we've run out of chairs. These gentlemen seated behind me are from the ad agency, and I'm Martin, your director." He half bowed with a wan flourish.

"Have a seat," he said, gesturing to the stool.

"Is that an ashtray?" I asked, pointing to the tall receptacle filled with chocolates.

"Not currently."

There had been no script provided, so I wondered what exactly they needed me to do.

"Okay, so what we're selling today is chocolate. You've seen the movie *When Harry Met Sally*?

"Yes."

"You know the scene where she fakes an orgasm?"

"Yes."

"Okay. Eat a piece of chocolate and do that."

"Fake an orgasm?"

"Yes. Unless you fancy having a real one." He chuckled odiously. The seventeen ad executives leaned slightly forward in their chairs.

"I'll need you to do it twice, once just normally, then make the second one bigger—that'll be used for the Netherlands market." I tried to digest this information.

"Um, do the Dutch really—"

"Look, just get on with it, will you, lovey? Tick-tock, et cetera."

I thought about all the girls waiting outside. All of us vying for an opportunity that was actually humiliation dressed up in a pick-me! outfit. I wanted to run out there and warn them. I wanted to tell them we were better than this, better than being lunchtime entertainment for a bunch of pervy execs, their perviness sanctioned by this being considered "work." But of course I didn't, because the fire was lit and it required fuel, and any fuel, however troubling, will burn just the same.

The chocolate was revolting, a feat of cocoa avoidance and ersatz sugar.

"Mmmm . . . mmmm, mmmm," I said, throwing my head around like Meg Ryan in Katz's Deli. I attempted her cries of "YES! YES! YES!"

"NYESH! NYESH! NYESH!" I gurgled, on account of the gumming agent used in the chocolate.

"That's it, "said Martin Scorsleazy, "really show us what that chocolate can do for you."

Beyond gagging, there was not much. I attempted a few more groans and seizures and then, realizing there was nowhere to spit out the chocolate, I did what so many women do in the name of pleasing men, and I swallowed.

"Okay, lovely, that was indeed lovely. Now let's see it again but remember this time do it bigger for the Dutch." I swiped my tongue across my teeth, trying to remove the vestiges of chocolate, to accommodate round two. The chocolate had shellacked my teeth with a hard, sweet, presumably brown finish.

"I don't think I can do it again," I said. The room snickered as one.

"'Course you can, love, that's the best bit about being a girl!" came a voice from the ad-men cabal.

I tried to keep my lips over my teeth as I began to speak

but then realized the audience actually deserved to see what they were promoting. My ambitious fire, that needed fuel, would have to go unfed.

"No, what I meant to say was I *won't* do it again because I will throw up." They thought I was talking about the chocolate, but it was really my shame at having gone along with the whole grotesquery. And the fucking chocolate.

Scorsleazy sneered and rolled his eyes. "Well, all of the other girls have apparently very much enjoyed this." I gathered the good coat I'd worn off the floor, smiled mightily, and said, "They were faking it."

As exits go, it wasn't bad. What was bad, I thought, as I walked back down Brewer Street, was the appearance of this line that would always be there. I could choose to cross or not cross, but either action would have practical and moral consequences. You speak up—they won't hire you. You don't speak up—you actually feel the good part of you begin to erode.

There was a message on my answering machine when I got home. "Oh, dear. Not very good reviews from the chocolate ad. They said you were difficult. Do call me and tell me what happened." My agent was lovely, she would always give me the benefit of the doubt, but I knew I'd now been marked, branded with the scarlet "D" that often comes with saying no as an actress.

The next few weeks were lean and spotted with other commercial auditions.

The Dog Food Commercial:

> INT. SOHO, DAY. A WINDOWLESS ROOM
> ABOVE A STRIP JOINT.
>
> BORED DIRECTOR
> Right, you're standing in a field of cows,
> they're gonna be dog food, they look
> delicious . . . and . . . ACTION!
>
> ME
> Mmmmmmmm, Dogchum,
> It's SOOOOOOOO beefy!

The Deodorant Commercial:

> INT. SOHO, EARLY EVENING.
> A WINDOWLESS ROOM ABOVE A SEX SHOP.
>
> BORED DIRECTOR
> Aaaand you're on the bus, you've had
> a sweaty day, you reach up for the strap
> to hang on to . . . aaaand, Oh, no, giant sweat

```
ring on your blouse, how embarrassing . . .
ACTION!
```

```
                    ME
Hands up if you use Sweat Guard,
Hands down if you don't!
```

The wind had dropped, the sails drooped, and the doldrums looked like they stretched to the horizon and even beyond. All the momentum gathered in making *Circle of Friends* seemed to have disappeared. I'd been the lead in a much-loved story and now I couldn't even book a fake orgasm. The winter was getting under way, and I'd had a terrible dream I was married to my heating bill. I called my sister to tell her about it. Calling her was something of an ordeal, as she and her boyfriend had moved from New York down to a small village outside Punta del Este in Uruguay. I had to call the post office and leave a message for her to call me back; it sometimes took a few days. The phone line crackled the following evening, and I could hear ambient Spanish in the background and the sound of crickets.

"Where exactly are you?" I asked her.

"In this village called La Barra. It's lovely, we're opening a shop." My sister sounded dreamy, which was very unlike her.

"What sort of shop?" I asked.

"A jeans shop."

"A what?"

"A jeans shop. A shop that sells jeans. Are you thick in the head?" The dreaminess had been dispatched.

"Willy had this great idea to get out of New York for the winter and to come down here and sell Levi's to all the rich Argentinians who show up in Punta del Este for the summer. We went and bought up all the used jeans in Brooklyn and shipped them down here. Willy says we are going to make a killing."

Willy was my sister's boyfriend, an Argentinian of few words with an enormous golden retriever called Juata (Wat-ah). I remember the dog more than him. Juata was one of those creatures who were clearly right on the verge of speaking when you talked to them. The kind of dog who would grab your sleeve and lead you to the stove when it was on fire or save your life when you were lost on a mountain pass by wrapping themselves around you through the night. The kind of dog that inspired myth. Willy, reflected in the light of his dog, came out very well.

"Is Juata down there with you?" I asked Kate.

"Yeah, of course. He's right here talking to the lady who sells watermelon. How's everything going in London?"

"Pear-shaped."

"I'm never exactly sure what that means. I like pears." She was back in dreamland.

"It *means* everything has sunk to the bottom. It *means* it's all sinking, and that it's heavy, and that shit's going DOWN."

It was unkind to want her to wake up to my gloom, but unfortunately it's written into the contract between sisters that if at any time, one party has grown too far apart from the other in terms of outlook, balance must be redressed by the happier one getting yelled at. I don't make the rules.

"Why don't you come down here?" she said calmly, refusing to be pulled into the abyss of my gloom-pear.

"You can work in the shop, and it's so cheap to live down here, and you can ride horses on the beach . . ." She drifted off, and I magnanimously let her. It sounded like a good idea. Everything was upside down where I was, so going to a place where it was summertime during the winter made sense. I needed to get away from who I wasn't, here in London. Fuck that whole, wherever-you-go-there-you-are philosophy. I was going to pull a geographical and go and be a seller of jeans in South America. I used my last two hundred pounds to buy a plane ticket to Montevideo and said adios to London for the winter.

La Barra, in the early nineties, was a sleepy village most of the year. It woke up in the summer months to welcome the rush of wealthy Argentinians who flocked to Punta del Este the way their European counterparts flocked to St. Tropez. The cab chugged along the coast for about eighty-five miles, from Montevideo to La Barra. I was white like a chrysalis in all the brightness and color and felt the hurrying chant inside my head, *quick! evolve, renew, fit in.* "Wherever you go there you are"—but not if I'm someone else.

We crossed the Arroyo Maldonado where the river meets the Atlantic and the brackish water was brown and churning and utterly foreign. La Barra had one main street with low adobe buildings and a hot wind that blew in off the Atlantic. I'd arranged to meet Kate at the post office, and the cab arrived in a cloud of dust and sand. I paid the driver and stood in the shimmering heat. Particles of the dirt road kicked up by the car and the wind swirled around—and there I was, a strange winter curiosity in my London parka, the center of a shaken snow globe, but instead of snow, dust.

A very suntanned blonde in a crocheted dress over a bikini wandered down the street.

"Christ, Min, take off your bloody coat." My sister was long and languid, she had always been the eternal Fay Wray to my gallumping King Kong. I took off my parka, and my arms glowed tourist white.

"Yeah, we need to get you a hat pronto, 'cause you're gonna burn like *carne de cerdo*."

"What's that?"

"Pork shoulder."

"Well, thanks a million, but I like pigs."

She grabbed my suitcase and began wheeling it down the road.

"Come on, come and see the shop."

I trailed after her automatically, a respite from the exhausting performance of leadership in my own life. Traipsing after Kate meant she was in charge, and as anyone who knew her would say, that is the best place for her to be.

We arrived outside a small storefront.

"Well, this is it. Isn't it great?" There was not a huge amount to recommend it from the outside: a window, a door, a broom leaning up against the door. It looked like every other small adobe structure on this part of the road.

"Come inside. It's even better!" We went in and apart from an enormous table with a mountain of jeans on it, there wasn't anything else.

"Isn't it great?" She beamed with delight.

"Yeah, it's good," I said.

Her face fell.

"Gosh, you don't have much imagination for a creative type, do you," she said, grabbing a pair of jeans and folding them neatly. She then gestured around the open space.

"We haven't opened yet. There are going to be shelves and a table for the cash register and there's a whole thing that happens this Saturday when everyone decorates the outside of their shop."

"Sorry. I couldn't really see beyond Mount Denim there. I'm sure it's going to be excellent."

She sniffed and said, "Get ready to do some serious work." I was happy to be employed.

She drove me out of town along a road that ran beside the ocean. After awhile we turned down a track that led to a small clearing in the middle of a grove of *pindos*—elegant palm trees that swayed gently in the breeze. The tiny cottage where Kate and Willy lived looked like it too might have been swaying but got frozen midway and now permanently listed to the right. Willy came cycling around the side of the house with Ouata balanced on the seat in front of him, the dog's paws braced against the handlebars.

"*Hola*, Minnie. *¿Qué tal?*" said Willy, although from where I stood, it looked like Ouata had said it.

The dog jumped off the bicycle and ran over to me, put his paws on my shoulders, and rested his nose between my ear and my neck.

"I am very well, thank you. How are you?" I replied. Ouata licked my chin, jumped down from our embrace, and ran into the house.

"You should go for a swim, Min, get the plane off you," said Kate. "I'll make some food."

I put on my swimsuit and slathered myself in zinc. It didn't seem possible for my skin to appear any whiter, but I'd managed it. I walked back along the track and emerged onto the coast road. There was nothing between it and the beach, just tarmac that disappeared into sand. There were no signs of people as far as the eye could see in either direction; it wasn't a destination beach but clearly somewhere you drove past on your way to one. The ocean looked gray and choppy but had no sign of any riptides, and a hot wind was blowing onshore.

Dive in, I thought, but I didn't. Instead, I stood there thinking about how many times I'd run away when things were hard. I'd done it physically and emotionally. This was the farthest I'd ever run, but it turned out that distance didn't change the fundamental truth. I braced myself and said out loud: "A woman never steps in the same river twice, for it is not the same river and she is not the same woman." I very much hoped this also applied to oceans.

In I dived. The cold water felt punitive: an Atlantic ocean fuck you for being equated with a river. Trying to find my breath in the cold, I concentrated on the space between strokes. A thought fired on the inhale: *surely repetition can make you stronger.* Another matched the exhale: *but wasn't repetition also some bumper sticker's definition of insanity?* The thoughts went in and out, creating a rhythm as if they were my own personal coxswain—a super-annoying coxswain.

I liked swimming parallel with the land; it felt like the land was a swimming buddy. I could go really long distances feeling its companionable presence. Swimming straight out is brilliant when you can see a destination: a rock, an island, the other side of a river. But when there's nothing but a vast plane of water, my reptilian brain called "foul!" Also, horizons were becoming thematic in my life, and I didn't want to contemplate another one.

I swam for about an hour, and when I flopped back onto the beach, was utterly exhausted. I must have fallen asleep because I woke up to a voice saying, "*Hola, Blanca.*" A man stood over me. He was mostly silhouette and very white teeth.

"It is the time for you to get off the sun."

I sat up and looked at my pinking skin, then back at the man. "Thanks. I fell asleep."

"Yes. It is good you are not able to steal from. You have nothing." He held out his hand.

"My name is Miguel. No trouble at all, you are welcome." Miguel spoke English in a kind, confident poetry of jumbled syntax. He escorted me back up the beach and seemed to know that I was staying with Willy and Kate in the leaning cottage.

"You are a long swim. I will take you to a faraway swim another morning. Don't sleep on the sun, *Blanca. Adios.*" He walked off back up the track that led to the road and a few minutes later, standing underneath the outdoor shower, I wondered if my jet lag had hallucinated him.

Kate had made rice and beans for dinner and we sat at the rickety kitchen table using tortillas as forks..

"Miguel follows the seasons," explained Willy. "He teaches snowboarding in Patagonia during the winter and surfing here in La Barra during the summer. He is a nice person for you to know, and he has a horse." The lights flickered slightly, and Willy cleared away the plates.

"The generator is low on oil. It is time for bed."

The tenterhooks upon which I'd been living faded and were replaced by a calm structure: swim, get off the sun, eat, electricity runs out, sleep. I lay in bed listening to the crickets, reflecting on the stark contrast between this life and the one I'd chosen. I knew I was in for big peaks and troughs as an actress, and the peaks would come only if I were really lucky. Navigating the troughs was really what I should train myself for. Maybe a person could learn to like a trough. I drifted off into dreams of horses riding across vast distances, scaling mountains and galloping across basins with equal ease.

The next few days were spent folding jeans and building shelving in the shop. The village was bustling with anticipation at the advent of the tourist season. At least four shop owners had heaved their ancient, brass cash registers onto the street, where they polished them with relish. The public polishing appeared to be a collective honoring of their most prized totem of cash. The woman with the biggest, heaviest cash register observed the others in triumph.

Kate had been right about how cheaply I could exist here. A pastry and a coffee, a few beers, some fish tacos, and a mango, all for about two dollars a day. *I could do this forever*, I thought on a long swim one afternoon. I could stay here and punt the previous life in favor of something simpler and less fraught. I don't have to be that thing; I could be this, a new coxswain had boarded the skull and the thoughts beat out a steady rhythm.

When the voice became too loud, I got out of the water on a lonely stretch of beach and faced the horizon. Having gradually been shedding the weight I'd gained for the character I played in *Circle of Friends*, I already looked like a different person. My tangle of hair was not out of place here on the beach, I could learn Spanish, I could want something else. It was late in the afternoon and I watched the ocean darken to a London gray. I could be this person—the thought shifted with the tide—I could pretend to be this person. But that was the immutable fact: I wanted to pretend to be *people*, not actually be someone else.

I remembered something the terrible person I'd once loved had said: "I dunno about reincarnation, but I do know that we live many lives in this one." It bothered me that I still thought about so many things he had said. That he had been wise as well as incredibly cruel were what made him terrible. It wasn't the good or the bad that was hard to metabolize, it was the polarity between the two. I'd done quite a lot of accommodating for his cruelty; it had chipped away at the part of me that believed I could feel sure about anything. Right as this memory began to fester, a figure on a white horse came galloping down the beach.

"*Hola, Blanca*" said Miguel as he brought the horse up just short of where I sat in the sand.

"*Hola, Miguel.*"

"You would want to go to a ride on us?"

"Yes, definitely. I'm soaking wet, though, and my T-shirt's back that way," I said, pointing down the beach.

"My T-shirt is here," he said, reaching down an arm and swinging me up behind him. We took off at a slow canter that opened up to a belting gallop as the beach flattened out ahead of us. *Wherever you go there you are. I am here*, I thought, and the "here" felt easier to understand than the "I."

Miguel rode me back home in the dark. I'd had my arms wrapped around him for practicality's sake but now hugged him with feeling. In the darkness, he had ridden in on a white horse and saved me, which was cool and also romantic. It was even better to know that the only saving I really needed was from my own thoughts.

"Thanks, Miguel, *gracias*," I said, hopping down. "I am so sorry I don't speak Spanish." I kissed the horse's soft nose and he stood very still and let me do it.

"The horse is the luck," Miguel said a bit ruefully, "with the kisses."

"The horse *is* the luck!" I replied. "See you tomorrow."

"See you tomorrow, *Blanca*. Tomorrow is a great day. You will see what the town will be. It will be many everything." Tomorrow was the day before the town fully opened. It was to be a day of great celebration.

"Can't wait," I said and waved as he rode his pale horse off into the night.

Kate woke me up early the next morning. We drank coffee from paper cups, and I shared my croissant with Ouata as we drove alongside the ocean and into the village. We pulled up and parked behind a long line of cars that had been left on the ocean side of the road. In the village, people milled around or stood in the middle of the road shouting orders. Laid out in front of all the storefronts, on the ground, appeared to be huge pieces of plywood. Holes were being drilled into the wood and brackets attached. We found Willy kneeling outside the shop threading rope through a bracket.

"Are you ready?" he said, tying off the rope and standing up. He called over to the woman with the shop next to us. She nodded at what he said and then in turn called over to the man next to her and on and on went the call and the curt nodded assents all the way down the street until there was no one left to nod to but a donkey standing in the shade of a eucalyptus tree.

"What is happening?" I asked Kate.

"You'll see. Put down your coffee, you'll need both hands." She stationed us in the middle of the road, facing the shop. Similar groups gathered in a long line, facing their shops. Willy and two other men were gathering the ropes attached to the wood laid on the ground. Everyone seemed to be holding their breath, waiting for some magic to happen. A man's deep, bass voice rang out.

"¡UNO. DOS. TRES, VAMOS A HACERLO!"

With whoops and shouts, the people on the ropes pulled

and the people in the middle of the road pushed. The giant pieces of plywood lifted off the ground; up and up they went, with the men hauling the ropes running backward down the sides of the shops, yelling for us to push harder. Kate and I, feet dug into the dirt, bodies at forty-five degrees, heaved and pushed until finally, triumphantly, the facade stood flush against the low, adobe shop. All along the street people clapped and cheered their new frontage. Back on the beach, behind the shops, the taut ropes were tied off to huge stakes, which were buried deep and sandbagged on top.

Our shop now had the appearance of being a two-story hacienda. A trompe l'oeil balcony ran along the second floor with vines and flowers tumbling down and framing the windows at street level. I wandered down the street, now transformed into a newly imagined place. Everyone had added a second or even third story to their shop. The store owner next to us had painted a sexy woman in a low-cut dress hanging off a balcony that was covered in bougainvillea. Planter boxes were painted on or below the windows and filled with a riot of flowers. The Virgin Mary and little toddler Jesus flanked the doorway, beckoning you to enter. The store owner pointed up to the sexy woman, *"Ese era yo a los 20."* (That was me at 20.) *"Yo estaba muy caliente."* (I was very hot.)

The grocery store, four doors down, had a full mariachi band on their second level, and speakers blasting out Mexican bangers. Transformation. Even the shop owners looked different: brighter, more vivid. There was nothing fake about the pretense, as if everybody had collectively agreed to be something else, even if it were only in appearance, and that there was to be celebration in that. The thing about being someone else for a living is that you (the actual person you are) run the risk of being discarded in favor of the shiny new mantle you are paid to step into. It offers a real possibility of having yourself described not just by the characters you play, but also by the inattention to your inner self. It felt dangerous and delicious to think of never having to excavate my own inner landscape in favor of ephemera.

I looked at the colorful, bigger-than-life facades as I walked down Main Street. I liked their glory. I liked the small adobe buildings they covered up too. Miguel appeared between two stores, walking up from the beach, leading his white horse.

"¡Hola, Blanca, que fiesta!" he said, leaning against the side of a shop, his head in line with the belt of a leering two-story cowboy—the centerpiece of the shop's "American West" theme.

"Hola, Miguel."

"You are looking like an 'uptown girl.'" He started singing "Uptown Girl" by Billy Joel. "I love Billy Joel—*el es un hero, el es un trovador.*" It was fun imagining Billy Joel as a troubadour, an eleventh-century medieval poet-singer roaming the world scoring the soundtrack for courtly love. But Miguel actually did see him as a version of this.

Miguel sang all the time. He sang on the mountains when he was snowboarding in Patagonia and when he was surfing the waves at Itacaré in Bahia, Brazil. He said he sang so his true love could find him. For him, people who sang and traveled were heroic, and love was the end game. That was his narrative, and he was as sure about it as I was unsure about mine.

"How do you know your true love is going to find you?" I asked him one day when he'd taken me for a ride miles and miles up the beach, almost to the town of José Ignacio. We sat under a palm tree, and his horse elegantly picked at the surrounding scrub.

"I know because I know," he said.

"Yes, but HOW do you know?" He looked at me quizzically, or with pity, or both.

"I know it because I *must* know it. If I am not doing the thinking first, how can the happen, happen for me?" It was simple: identify what you want, think about it, wait for it to manifest.

I was annoyed by the simplicity. "But you can't just think about something and then it happens," I said.

"Why? That is how all the things work."

"Not for me."

"Not for yet."

"Well, who is in charge of the timeline?" He looked perturbed. I thought he didn't understand the word, so I went on: "The timeline, the itinerary, the order of business, who says *when*?"

He continued looking at me. Then said very slowly, as though to a child or a person who was unfamiliar with simple concepts, "I understand what you are saying. *You* do not understand that 'timeline' is not a good idea to be thinking about. Think about what you want and then forget about it, maybe sing, maybe go for a surf, maybe enjoy the Billy Joel with your amigo Miguel." He smiled and started singing "Piano Man" very loudly. His horse looked up sharply at the noise, then realizing it was just "Piano Man" and not something more sinister, went back to the salty grass.

I squinted up at my serenading friend, full of life, full of enjoyment, full of wisdom and Billy Joel. Everything felt so much more complicated to me, and even as I thought it, I realized that if I didn't want complicated, I'd better at least stop saying it was so.

"Miguel, I want a beer and a job."

"A beer and a job!!! *¡Bueno, bueno!* You know what you want, I am relieved like fuck!"

"Me too. Sort of. I mean at this point I'm literally just saying it."

"Whatever. Fake it till you are make it." We stood, stretched, and got back on his horse.

"You're a solid friend, Miguel." He urged the horse into a canter and maybe as a full stop to our conversation, or just because it felt good, he started singing "It's Still Rock and Roll to Me."

Weeks later, maybe months, the glassy hot, blue sky days, by their unbroken continuity, had dispensed with timelines altogether. Kate's shop was open seven days a week and you'd only know it was Sunday because the lone bell in the church would ring. I was standing in the shop one morning, idly staring out the window at the ocean, folding jeans. I was dreaming of all the things I wanted, not with the desperation of the unfulfilled, but almost as though they had already happened, and I was remembering them. The jeans folding was the mudra, the thoughts were the meditation. As a gaggle of Argentinian boys exploded through the door—laughing and chatting, Ray•Bans on, collars popped on their pastel-hued golf shirts, like one giant Benetton ice cream—Miguel's head appeared through the ocean-facing window.

"*Blanca*, telephone for you at L'Oficina de Correos. Go, I will watch *los chicos*." I thanked him and hurried out of the store. It was probably my mother, and I was going to try and convince her to come down here and fold jeans with us. As I picked up the phone in the post office the line crackled mightily when I said hello. My agent's voice shouted across the Atlantic.

"Love, can you hear me?!"

"Yes."

"Okay, well, if you can hear me, I have good news."

"I can hear you."

"Not sure you can hear me, but they want to see you for the Bond film."

"WHAT?!"

"I said they want you to go and see them about the new Bond. Don't get too excited, you don't kill anyone or shag anyone so technically—not a Bond girl, but I still think you should come back."

The line crackled, I crackled, and then it was all clear.

"Do you think it's worth my coming back for just a chance?"

"Oh goodness, there you are. A chance? Well, what on earth else do you want?"

6

A WEEKEND AWAY

My agent called me at the end of January.

"I think you should go to New York."

"Why am I going to New York?"

"Because *Circle of Friends* is coming out in a few months and I am sensing this would be a good moment for you to go and introduce yourself to some casting directors and for you to meet with American agents."

"Okay. Sounds good. One problem: I don't have any money to buy a plane ticket or pay for a hotel or any food." My agent sighed.

"What exactly do you *do* with the money you earn, Minnie?"

"I spend it. I get excited that I have it, and then I spend it."

"What do you spend it on?"

"Well, last week, with the last of the *GoldenEye* cash, I took everyone to San Lorenzo for dinner."

"Who's 'everyone'?"

"Twenty of my nearest and poorest."

"You can't afford to take twenty people to San Lorenzo!" she shouted.

"Not anymore I can't!" I shouted back.

After a moment's impasse she said,

"Okay. I'm going to lend you the money and you are going to pay me back when you get your next job."

"You're very nice to me."

"I know. But you are basically a high-risk investment and I'm just choosing to ride the fluctuations of the market until it stabilizes."

A week later, the evening before I left, my mother came over for dinner.

"There's no food," I said as I opened the door. "I spent the last food money on tights for New York."

"Don't worry, I bought fish," she said, pulling a packet of fish out of her bag.

"It's halibut," she murmured conspiratorially, in the same way some people say "It's Dior."

"Ah no, Mum! No! Not fish! It stinks the place out when you cook it, and my hair will reek on the plane!"

"Stop complaining and put your hair in a towel. This fish is delicious and *so* good for us." She barged in and headed upstairs to the tiny galley kitchen and proceeded to fry the halibut. I ran around opening windows, hair in a towel, wishing she didn't have such a bizarre relationship with food. Whenever my mother would gain a few pounds, she would start eating oranges, and only eat oranges until the extra pounds were gone. At fifteen I'd been in the throes of adolescence; I'd had mild acne and had put on a fair bit of weight. I went to my mother that summer and asked for her help:

"Can we eat healthier, Mum?" She started to point toward the fruit bowl, but I cut her off.

"Don't say 'Eat oranges'!"

The next morning, I came downstairs and saw that there were new decorations all over the kitchen. Detailed, pen-and-ink drawings of skulls and crossbones, with the word "poison" underneath them, had been painstakingly drawn onto large adhesive stickers, the stickers had then been slapped onto anything my mother thought we should avoid: the cereal box, the bread bin, the cookie jar, the fridge itself. She always said that the war and rationing—having turned most food into contraband on the black market—had ruined her ability to figuratively metabolize it in a sane way. I agreed.

After dinner she came and sat on the bed in my room as I packed.

"How long are you going for?"

"Get there Friday, stay Saturday, Sunday, then leaving Monday night."

She looked over my suitcase:

- 2 pairs of jeans
- 4 T-shirts
- 1 denim skirt
- 1 Amishy dress
- 1 stripper dress
- 1 pair of Nike Cortez trainers
- 1 pair of high heels
- 5 pairs of knickers
- 1 pair of tights

My mother noticed I hadn't packed any bras.

"You're not coming back, are you?" I didn't understand her lingerie divination.

"'Course I am!" She sighed and smiled and tucked a couple of oranges underneath my T-shirts and said quietly,

"Just for the road."

New York was blisteringly exciting. Philippe Starck had designed the tiny hotel room I was staying in, and every time I banged my elbow on the infinite number of sharp edges in that room, I felt a jolt of electrical energy that seemed to be more than just my shrieking funny bone. I wandered up and down the avenues and across the streets until I had hit the river on both sides. New York appeared real, and of itself. It didn't have the first date thrill of a Rome or a Paris, whose darker underbellies were fronted by the grace and culture of a thousand years, their first impressions beautifully presented in the architecture of the churches and piazzas. There, you might be seduced and beckoned into the arms of locals with an ancient promise of romance. New York presented itself as the eccentric old person your lover had grown into, with a refusal to compromise that was underlined by every streetside urination, screaming fight, and bucket of fish guts thrown out across the cobblestones and onto your one pair of trainers. I was in love.

On the afternoon of my arrival, I hurried to the offices of the casting director, Ellen Lewis. Owing my entire career thus far to the generosity of a British casting director, I had an extreme reverence for them as a whole. Ellen had cast *Casino* and *Forrest Gump*, and it was with extreme nervousness that I climbed the stairs to her office in my fish-gut trainers and waited outside.

She was incredibly nice and didn't mention the strong odor of fish. We chatted and she asked me questions about work. I had nothing to really talk about except this film, *Circle of Friends*. She had heard a bit about it, but it, like me in New

York, was still conceptual at this point. I told her I was in the new Bond film, and just as I was about to qualify that my part amounted to roughly forty-five seconds of screen time, two male voices started shouting from the room next door. We carried on chatting, pretending there was no shouting for as long as we could, then when the shouting became an almost monk-like chant of the word "fuck," Ellen excused herself and said she would be right back.

I heard her go into the office next door, yell briefly at whoever was in there, and then all was quiet. In the silence of this kind stranger's office, I felt the reawakening of the idea I'd had in Uruguay—I can be anyone here and no one would know because I have no imprint here at all. Who will I be? I was struck by the familiar, now slightly vertiginous feeling I got when I realized it might really be the right time to ditch all of who I was and start again. Immediately feeling guilty about having so little loyalty to myself, I stared out the window and was soothed by the anonymity of all the hurrying people on the street below. *It feels so good to be a blank slate*, I told myself. The block of marble with the statue inside, waiting to be re-vealed. Like the shouting, I politely ignored the statue already in existence.

Ten minutes later Ellen put her head around the door.

"I've had a thought," she said. "Would you be up for meeting a couple of directors?"

"Sure," I said. "When?"

"Now. Next door."

"The shouters?"

"Yes." I must have looked worried because she then said,

"Don't worry, they really don't shout all the time. Their movie begins in a week and the actress they had cast just fell out. I don't know, I just think you should meet them."

"Well, okay, thank you, but is the part British?"

"No, she's from Jersey. Can you do an American accent?" The new statue spoke for me.

"Yes, definitely."

I went next door to meet the shouters. They were warm, bemused by my being completely unknown to them, polite, but clearly unconvinced that the girl they needed for their film would have just happened to be waiting in the office next to them. There was a certain urgent desperation about the two of them, though, and maybe serendipity was the only thing that was going to distract them.

"So how long have you been in New York?" said one of the men.

"Sixteen hours."

"Sixteen? Aren't you tired of it yet?" The other one took over: good cop/good cop.

"We are making a movie that has a lot of food in it. Do you like to eat?"

"Yes."

"A lot?"

"Well, I *can* eat a lot, but I have to have the right pants on."

We went on like this for a while: me joking, them assessing. I couldn't believe they were buying the plausibility of my being in their film, but I was just along for the ride and my new statue seemed to be dealing with all the turns it was taking. I had a new bravado, an ease I didn't usually feel. I had nothing to lose but myself and it felt dangerous but inevitable.

I walked back up Broadway when the strange, impromptu meeting was over, and across Forty-Sixth Street, past my hotel, until I was standing looking out over the Hudson, where about fifty people were waiting to get on a Circle Line sightseeing cruise. The crowd was made up of large groups of friends and families, some groups wore the same T-shirt, some took pictures of the others, with the river as a backdrop and beyond it, Weehawken, New Jersey, glinting in the distance. They were known in an unknown city, aliens dropped into a landscape they wanted to play in for a while and then leave.

In the afternoon I went to the William Morris Agency to meet with some agents. Getting ready for the meeting at the hotel I had put on my Amishy dress, as Kelly McGillis in *Witness* was always a solid fashion reference. But looking at my reflection in the mirror I realized a blank canvas was probably a better image to project than abstinence-chic. I changed immediately into my jeans and a white T-shirt.

Waiting in the large conference room, I let my intimidation be cheered by the fact that you can't worry that you might be an impostor if you actually are one. The door opened and I was greeted by a smile of agents. They had short hair and gray suits, baring teeth, and outstretched hands. I stood up and the man who reached me first shook my hand and said,

"You're tall. Isn't she tall? . . . NOT what I was expecting!" The rest of the gang smiled more and agreed.

"You dress casual and you're THIN! Good Lord, did you put on all that weight for the movie? How d'you lose it? Was it Atkins, Pritikin, the South Beach?"

"Lack of funds, actually."

"'Lack of funds' hahaha! That's great, you have a great sense of humor." Now it was my turn to smile aggressively because I didn't know what else to do.

"Well, we LOVE you, we think you're just TERRIFIC." The other man nodded. "How long are you in town?"

"Just until Monday."

"We want to invite you to a party tomorrow night and introduce you to some folks. That'd be great, right?"

"Yes. Great!"

"I smell big things, missy!"

"You do?"

"Yup. You are NOT what we expected." This was apparently good, as I too was not what I had expected. I wondered how close my version came to theirs.

"What did you expect?"

"Oh, a shorter, more homely girl—a character actress, perhaps. But you are leading Ladyville!"

"Do you think I could pass for an American?" His smile faltered for a second, I think he thought it might be a test, but I really just wanted to know how far I could go with being someone else.

"Uh, sure, why not? You don't want to be British?"

"No, I like being British, I just wondered if I could fit in here, in America."

"Even better!—you can fit in AND break the mold! How about that, huh? How ABOUT that?"

It was exactly the right amount of incoherence I needed—it was vague and shiny and a lot to do with how I looked; a relatable cadence for an insecure personality. I said my good-byes and they told me where the party was the following night. All the next day in between more meetings with nice people who asked me questions about my life, my hair, my accent, and how I lost weight, I walked through New York. Anonymity and definition. I was anonymous until circumstances described me. A cab almost hit me—I yelled at it with an American accent. Construction workers catcalled my ass as I walked by, and I yelled at them in French. There was a curious freedom in trying on new identities. I wondered if I had quietly gone mad and knew my sister would know if I had. I called her from a pay phone on the corner of Fourteenth Street.

"I'm pretending to be other people and I like it."

"Isn't that what acting *is*?"

"Yes, but in real life I'm doing it."

"Why are you doing that? That's fucking bonkers."

"Feels free."

"Well, what on earth is unfree about being yourself?"

"I dunno. My history, it weighs on me."

"Your history?" She said it very much like Lady Bracknell says "A haaaandbaaaag?" in *The Importance of Being Earnest*.

"I just feel like this is a real chance to be someone else legitimately. Nobody knows anything about me here, except that I was a size fourteen in *Circle of Friends* and now I'm not. They don't know and they don't care. I could start again and do it better because I'll be paying more attention this time, because I know I'm getting a second chance. I can consciously decide who I am and not let circumstance or previous damage dictate it, I can be the conscious architect of my own life!"

"You sound bat-shit crazy and really pretentious," said my sister.

I sighed. I wasn't explaining it well enough, or she really didn't get it.

"There's nothing wrong with who you are, Min."

"But it's uncomfortable."

"That," she said, "is unavoidable, whoever you are."

I hung up and wondered why she would vouch for discomfort so vociferously. I felt like I could stay one step ahead of everything painful if I wasn't burdened by identifying with it. Here I was in the evolution of the idea I had toyed with while living in Uruguay—that you could shed your old self like a snake's skin, and birth yourself into someone new. The self-midwifery angle suddenly cast worrying shadows of narcissism, but I skipped over them like Red Riding Hood on her way to Grandma's. Nothing bad could happen.

That evening, I put on my stripper dress and towering heels and wobbled into the street to hail a cab. The party was at the home of one of the big agents at William Morris. At the door, the butler offered to take my coat. I thanked him and he said,

"You're English."

"Yes," I said, "but maybe not for long!" He pointed to himself and said kindly,

"Bournemouth! But I've been here twenty-five years, it's not that hard to hang on to."

"Do they like you more because you're British?" I asked,

"Well, it suits the job, doesn't it? I probably would have

gotten an American accent years ago if they all hadn't seen *The Remains of the Day* and wanted a British butler like Anthony Hopkins."

"But he's Welsh."

The butler sniffed, "It's all the same to an American ear."

I pointed to the smart livery he was wearing.

"Does the dressing up help?"

"Oh yes, the dressing up is 90 percent of why I like it."

"Me TOO," I said excitedly.

"Well, you'd better go in, dear." He was very nice about telling me to scram.

In the party, I was the tallest person by a solid head and shoulders, and the huge mirror hanging over the fireplace reflected a colorful giant in a sea of suits. I immediately saw that the dress code was business casual and thought I would have fitted in perfectly if they'd all casually come to my strip club after work. It was good, though, as I was easily spotted by the group of agents I'd met the previous day and they swept me off to meet Al Pacino, who was doing a play they said I was perfect for. Al Pacino appeared before me like a familiar dream.

"Hiya, Al, how are you?" said the agent who seemed to speak for all of them.

"Oh, you know, still tryna make a dollar out of ninety-nine cents."

"Hahaha, oh. Al, that's funny, that is FUN-NEE."

Al Pacino smiled and I blinked my eyes to take a mental picture of him.

"Al, there is someone we would like to introduce you to, we think she's very special, she's got a movie coming out that is HOT, she's a real chameleon, you're gonna love her." I was thrust forward, and as I gazed down into Al Pacino's limpid, brown eyes, I tried not to scream. The speaker agent said,

"This is Mandy, Mandy Dreyfus."

"Hi, Mandy, very nice to meet you," said Al Pacino.

There was a moment when I could have corrected him, but it passed. She had a name: "Mandy."' The agents LOVED her, Al Pacino now knew her, she had been fully born and christened wearing a gaudy, inappropriate dress. It was perfect. Everything that happened so fast and so furiously in the next few years ricocheted off this moment and deftly illustrated the root of my ambition and desire, which was to be seen and unseen.

My agent in London called me on Monday morning.

"You got the part in the film I had no idea about."

"Did I? That is *so* weird. I wasn't even trying. Did Ellen Lewis tell you how I met the directors?"

"She did. Very odd. Just an unbelievable stroke of luck."

"For them."

"For you."

"Yeah, but as *my* agent, more for them, right?"

"I'm glad to hear you're feeling more confident about yourself," she said dryly.

"Oh, it's not me. But it makes things easier."

"Well, it's very exciting. They start shooting next week so you won't be coming home. Have you got the right clothes?"

I thought about Mum being tipped off by my lack of bras, and my terrible, flammable dress from the party. I thought about the new clothes I'd now buy, ones that would tell a story that didn't need the provenance of my body to be understood. Clothes that just looked like I'd always been this thin and this cool.

"Yeah, I think I'm good," I said.

7

YOU'RE IT

Becoming famous was like everyone else had taken hallucino-genic drugs and I was the giant talking mushroom in their trip. It was hardly noticeable at first, people would smile in my direction sometimes, but it could have been at something happening be-hind me; then the next thing I knew, a guy was lying in the gutter as I'd get out of my car, trying to take a picture of my vagina.

Fame—the caboose to the engine of my wanting to act—presented a psychological paradox that was unexpected: wanting to be seen, but not that much.

Nobody had much sympathy, and in the press, there were echoes of that pernicious qualifier of a woman's experience of unwanted attention, passed down through the ages in a vicious relay:

"Well, she was asking for it, wasn't she?"

I had been living and making movies in New York, staying mostly in hotels and on couches. For a few nights I had slept in my tiny dressing room on the Chelsea Piers, where we were shooting the film *Big Night*. The best thing about this was waking up at 5:30 a.m. and going and sitting at Isabella Rossellini's feet and watching her put on her makeup. Drowsy from the hour and the August heat, I listened as she told me stories of Italy and of being on sets with her mother. Her beautiful voice would lull me further back to sleep, until eventually my head would rest against the leg of her chair and the silky trail of her kimono.

My sister found my living situation "needlessly uncomfortable" and told me that some friends of friends she'd had in college were looking for a roommate.

Bill was Diane Keaton's assistant and Alexandra was a photographer turned writer. Both had grown up in Washington, DC, had known each other a long time, and were a double act of the Mike Nichols/Elaine May variety.

"We don't mind if you pay more and have a bigger room. You're an actress, you *should* pay more, you *should* have a bigger room," said Bill.

"Yeah, I'll sleep in the closet as long as the lighting's good," said Alexandra.

We spoke on the phone, and I asked her how we would find an apartment.

"I'll get up really early and get the *Times*. I can always find apartments. It's a gift I can't monetize, which blows, but we're gonna live somewhere awesome."

"Couldn't you be a Realtor," I said, "to monetize your gift?" There was a long silence.

"Yeah, but then I'd have to be a Realtor."

The very next day she called me at 7:00 a.m. and told me to go meet the landlord of the place she'd found.

"Take cash for the deposit and I'm pretty sure your British accent will work instead of a credit score."

I arrived a few hours later at a brownstone on Twenty-Second Street, between Ninth and Tenth Avenues. It was a ground and first-floor apartment with two bedrooms and a huge bay window onto the street. The landlord took the cash, I signed some grubby papers, then she gave me the keys and said,

"Rent is first of the month, Ethan Hawke lives down the street—DON'T BOTHER HIM. The Ha Ha deli on Ninth Avenue is good for gin and cigs—BUT DON'T EAT THEIR SANDWICHES." Then she left, and I quickly looked out the window for Ethan Hawke. Our super, a man named Claude, disapproved of us immediately. He had the air of the proprietor of a ladies' boardinghouse from the nineteenth century, and clutched imaginary pearls under his overalls every time a new lover emerged at daybreak onto our stoop. When my bedframe broke and I asked if he could help me fix it, he took a long time shaking his head "no"—

apparently I had made my own bed from sin and now I must lie in it.

I was making the movie *Sleepers* and sometimes would ride my bike to the set, often trailed by paparazzi—also on bikes. I was younger, fitter, and very much enjoyed forcing them to race down the West Side Highway. Occasionally I would flash them my knickers as some kind of fuck you for the picture they couldn't get without heading into oncoming traffic. The movie had virtually every famous actor I'd ever heard of in it. I watched them jostle for their hierarchical positions and wondered how it got decided. It was thrilling in the extreme to have been included, but the truth was I was eminently cuttable. A two shot with Brad Pitt would go like this:

"Okay, A-camera got the two of you in a medium and B-camera is a bit closer. Okay, Minnie, just take a small step, camera left [a short conversation would then take place behind the monitors], OKAAAAAY, and another step [more chat], ALRIGHTY, and one more step left, please, Minnie [silence]."

"OKAY, IT'S A SINGLE ON BRAD, PEOPLE . . . MAKEUP!"

I had one scene with Robert De Niro, and it was the only time we ever really rehearsed anything but the blocking. I didn't say anything in the scene, and he gave me one of his own lines, which felt like receiving the sacrament.

I was terrified and never knew what to call him. Everyone called him Bob, but I couldn't call Robert De Niro "Bob." On the set I used to cough before I'd speak to him, which would generally get his attention (if make him jump a little). He was very kind and very calm and one day gave me a box of cough drops.

"You gotta deal with that cough."

"Yes [cough]."

Our set, as a place to come and visit and hang out, was a revolving door of movie luminaries. I once had a close-up where all I could see in my line of vision was Martin Scorsese eating a sandwich. I watched every actor with hawkish intensity, fascinated by how each closed the distance between the written lines and their performance once the cameras were rolling. At night I'd study the scenes for the following day, not my own part, but those of all the others, and I'd try to imagine what the different actors would do. The next day I would hang around and watch all the scenes I'd read the night before and take mental notes on performances. I listened to the direction Barry Levinson would give and then saw how those notes were either metabolized into the performance or ignored completely.

Barry was incredibly easygoing and when faced with one actor's rancorous disagreement about a scene and its blocking, he smiled and listened to the actor's ideas. The actor wanted to change a lot of the dialogue because he'd woken up that day and apparently realized his character wouldn't say what was written. I'd met the guy for breakfast earlier, ostensibly to discuss the movie, and we had been ushered past the people waiting in line, and seated, just the two of us, at a table for six.

"How do you know your character wouldn't say what's written?" I asked.

"Instinct," said the actor.

"But how come you didn't know it before, like, all the other times you've read the script?"

"I didn't get the message until today."

This sounded very witchy and right up my street, frankly—messages from the Muse arriving just in the nick of time?!—but it also sounded like something else I couldn't quite put my finger on, some kind of excuse.

Back on the set, the other thing the actor needed Barry to do was get rid of all the track laid down for the camera move—he said it distracted him and that anyway, the camera should be locked off and static, because that was a truer reflection of his character's "inflexibility." The actor braced himself for the resistance he thought must be coming, but Barry seemed disinclined to fight and after a quick chat with the producer agreed to what the actor wanted; he did, though, ask rather genially if it would be okay to shoot a big, wide shot from across the street, and the actor said that yes, that would be fine by him.

In the annals of successful conflict resolution while avoiding compromise of your own creativity—and even though I guess it's not a competition—Barry won.

When the movie came out and I watched the scene in question, all the dialogue had been replaced by music and the whole scene played out in the one big, wide shot from across the street. I had learned a key lesson as an actor: if you want to do battle on a set, you must make peace with the fact that the war will still most likely be won by someone else. Also, a six top for only two of you is lame.

When I wasn't working, Alexandra and I hung out in a place on Ninth Avenue called Les Deux Gamins and surreptitiously watched Ethan Hawke write his first novel. We both took a picture of him staring out the window, lost in thought, and I told her we were starting to behave like idiots.

"Oh yeah, yeah," she said. "But if he turns out to be a writer and not a movie star and we didn't get a picture of him doing it . . . WELL, WHO ARE THE IDIOTS *THEN?*"

"Still us," I said.

I couldn't get enough of watching actors at work, on the set or in the theater. There was something hypnotic about seeing people do the same thing I did and trying to figure out exactly how they were doing it—a contradictory narcissism that wanted to explore the outer reaches of possibility, but only insofar as it related to me.

One night I was invited by my friend Rufus to see the play *Indiscretions* on Broadway. His friend was starring opposite Kathleen Turner and somehow when the play was over, we had wound up in her dressing room, sitting on the floor with our knees up to our chins, watching this legend receive her well-wishers. I thought she had been magnificent in the play, her voice so loud and commanding counterbalanced by incredibly nuanced emotion. Jude Law (Rufus's friend) had also been electrifying, causing maximum ruffle throughout the entire auditorium as he appeared completely naked.

"Isn't being naked onstage, like, TOO real?" I asked Rufus. "I mean, he was brilliant in that play but all anyone is talking about is his penis."

"I wouldn't mind if that's all people talked about me," said Rufus, "and anyway, as long as they're talking about you—"

"But what about acting?" I said, miffed that notoriety and/or penises should get the upper hand.

"I am going to make a very bad pun now," replied Rufus. "An actor is the sum of his parts. Sometimes his flesh parts."

"Gross," I said. "But please tell me more about the *nuts and bolts* of our profession."

As we sat watching Kathleen Turner chatting to her friends, there was a sudden commotion outside, in the hallway. The door to her dressing room opened and a frisson of electricity entered, followed by Lauren Bacall. The two megalodames viewed each other across the distance of their outstretched arms, their halfway smiles reaching out, but just falling short.

"Are they acting?" I whispered to Rufus.
"I have no idea," he whispered back.

I watched Lauren Bacall, unhurried, basking in the run-up to her hello. I wondered if she was Kathleen Turner's mentor, if they were great friends; I racked my brain for a movie they might have been in together. I couldn't believe I was going to be witness to one legend's appraisal of another's performance. I thought I was about to receive the holy grail of acting notes and l could barely breathe for the excitement.

"BETTY," said Kathleen Turner.

"KATHLEEN TURNER," purred Lauren Bacall, "ON-STAGE."

And that was it.

Alexandra was making coffee one morning and we had run out of filters.

"I'll run to the Ha Ha deli and get some," I said.

"There're photographers outside so you'll need to put something fancy on," she replied.

"Is this it?" I said. "Is this something I now have to take seriously—that I'm genuinely considering taking off my pajamas, putting on a dress and makeup, to make sure I don't look bad for the buzzards outside?"

"Yeah," said Bill. "People do that every day at this time of the morning. It's called 'getting ready to go to work'. . . ."

"So this is work now?—have an identity shift to accommodate the creepy paps and to keep myself nice and aspirational for all the tabloid readers?"

"Yes, part of it," he said, looking over the top of his tabloid, "but perception, not identity, image, not identity. Just curate what they see and hang on to the rest of you."

"But that's it," I said, sitting on the kitchen floor sifting through a huge box of beautiful clothes that had arrived from

Gucci the previous day. I held up a pale pink suede strapless column of a dress. "I feel very little loyalty to the person I actually am—untidy, overemotional, insecure—and when I look at a dress like this I would much rather be the dress."

"Aw, honey, you're not so bad," said Alexandra, not having been able to wait for the coffee and now using her bra as a filter. "You're you on the inside."

I wondered if the me on the inside might be left to shrivel up as I more closely aligned myself with the dress and all it represented in its perfectly tailored way.

"But they don't want any insides," I said, pointing out the window at the paps. "Those assholes want outsides."

"Acting wants your insides, movies want that," ventured Bill.

"But isn't a person supposed to be kinda more . . . whole? Don't you think I might start making bad decisions if it's just one little disconnected piece making the decision?"

They both looked at me.

"You are waaaaaay overthinking this," said Bill.

"Here, have a B cup of coffee," said Alex.

I wore all the dresses and held the bags. In photos I tried to leave my face in neutral, but it came across as more beatific zombie. In restaurants, cabs, elevators, shops, people were always glad to see me—this person I didn't recognize—and they intimately told me all the things I made them feel, they said they felt like they knew me; and I couldn't quite get a fix on who that was. Meanwhile, the press in the UK eviscerated this other person

I didn't know, who was also me. They said she was ruthlessly ambitious and pushy and thought herself too good for England. I wondered about her a lot and felt quite sorry for her. It was all so divorced from the reality I was experiencing, but there it was in newsprint, some newly deployed empirical truth.

In the movie *Grosse Pointe Blank* that following spring, John Cusack told me to just be myself when I admitted feeling lost among the cast he'd put together of sharp, fast-talking boys whom he'd grown up with.

"Which version?" I asked him and I think he thought I was kidding.

"Pick one," he said with a grin.

Bill was heading back to California with Diane Keaton, and Alexandra found out her boyfriend had been cheating on her with a slew of women.

"God," she said, hands on hips, shaking her head. "What a *dummy*."

"You are so not a dummy," I said.

"What? Oh God no, not me, *him*." She was incredibly grounded for such a free spirit. Part of her was casting around for what she creatively wanted to do in her life, and her patchouli oil, her flowy, Indian print dresses, and her wild, long black hair were a misdirect away from her clear focus and genius humor about life.

"Min, I gotta get out of here. I'm gonna go to LA. I think you should come too."

"What, just move?"

"Yeah."

"But didn't we just get here?"

"Yeah. But that's a terrible reason to stay."

"But what if it gets better?"

"Honey, we are not getting any younger." (We were barely twenty-five.)

"Okay, well, I don't want to stay here without you, so I'll come. When would we go?"

"Book a flight. There're tons of places we can stay till I find our California dream duplex. I feel like everyone lives in a duplex there until they have shitloads of cash."

I did not know what a duplex was, I only knew that heading west was the next logical step, if only to avoid going east and home.

"I have an audition on Friday," I told her.

"Okay, well, let's scram next week then."

The audition in question had come from a script the man I'd been dating had slipped me. The script had been given to him by a producer named Chris Moore, who shared office space in the same building where they both worked. I called my agent when I'd read it.

"Oh, yeah, that's a hot script. How did you get it?" she said.

"Oh, long story. Can you get me in?"

"I will try." My American agent was new to me, honest and Irish.

The script was gripping and funny and sad. The female role felt underwritten, but as that was the case with every female role out there, it didn't really bother me. There was space in the writing, in the breadth of the characters; you could feel like there was room to grow. I sat around for days reading the scenes, I played all the characters in different bits that I liked, learned their lines, said the words out loud. It was easy learning the scenes for the audition—good writing goes in and a strong foundation is set. With this girl, in this movie, all there was to do, then, was play.

I arrived at The Mercer hotel for my audition and was shown to the director Gus Van Sant's suite, where it would be taking place. He was charming and quiet and quickly said all the others would be showing up soon. We sat around. We did not chat. He grew increasingly embarrassed as time dragged on and apologized profusely. I didn't care at all. All of this was weird-and-awkward: New York, being chased by paparazzi, having Brad Pitt stroke my hair in a scene on the subway, and being metabolized by everyone as a person I didn't recognize. Hanging around waiting for other actors and a producer to show up felt relatively normal, but I could see it made Gus very uncomfortable. Eventually, after about an hour, the door opened and a group of men spilled in. They were a riot of apology. Something to do with a broken foot, and cabs, and something else or other. I looked at the two young guys in the group whom I knew were the writers. They were incredibly sorry and quite hung over.

Waiting around to audition can do two things: (1) Your nerves can dissipate all the juicy focus you arrived with and, as the clock ticks on, you may watch that focus sail away on the receding tide of adrenaline it came in on; (2) Waiting around *doesn't* dissipate your focus, but obversely, keeps distilling it more and more, clarifying it until you could sit there forever (or until they called your name), completely sure and settled in what you're going to do.

I was not nervous at all; I was stoked and happy. This script was brilliant, I could play the part standing on my head, and everybody else was superflustered, which gave me the space to just sit and wait while they all calmed down.

The scene they wanted to do from the movie was a big emotional fight scene between the two young lovers. I had been in this scene in my life; something that starts somewhere intimate and loving, but at some point an unwitting word or question triggers a nuclear meltdown. It was not a stretch. We launched into the scene and, sharpened by waiting and eager to be into this next bit, I was more on top of things than Matt, the writer/actor acting opposite me; he looked a bit queasy and was reaching for the words. Forty seconds in and Matt called a time-out.

"Hold on. Sorry. This is nuts, you are right in this and I'm not, and I don't want to fuck you up, so would you mind if I just took a minute?"

I fell in love with at least part of him in that moment. Self-awareness and generosity had always been beguiling for me. But as he shuffled off to collect himself, I also felt a rush of love for my young self—for feeling powerful in an apparently disempowered situation.

When he returned, he was fully present and the scene became fierce play, and satisfyingly, made everyone watching cry by its end. We were all made friends by this experience; the chaos coming into focus, their words coming off the page and having life breathed into them with undeniable impact. It was a good beginning for us.

A few days later our good beginning hit a brick wall when the word came down from Harvey Weinstein, whose studio was producing the film, that they could not cast me because, as he told everyone involved, "Nobody would want to fuck her."

I took great exception to hearing this, as I had a list that, while not very long, was full of quality people who definitely would've liked to have a go. I was also stunned that a man such as Harvey Weinstein—whose shirts were always aggressively encrusted with egg/tuna fish/mayo, who terrified and revolted in equal measure, and who lived within a cloud of yellowed cigar smoke—was any kind of arbiter for what or who was fuckable.

It was with immense satisfaction that hot on the heels of hearing about my apparent sexual incapacity, word came that both the writers and the director would not make the film without me. I was fully aware that they *would* have made the film without me, but being so vocally championed by a group I had just met felt like a sign that they were just the sort of people I would like to be devoted to.

Making something with a person you admire, bringing it to life and making it tangible, can feel like love. Finding out how they came to be admirable—meeting their family, seeing how beloved they are by their friends, watching their curiosity in real time make it real. I was aware that with a few previous men, I had worked very hard to be the emotional grout for all their fractured pieces. Matt appeared to me whole and connected. I ignored the fact that we were both actors—a compatibility that rarely goes the distance. My heart set on his horizon and I was pretty much done for. Our love story played out alongside the movie, and when it didn't end along with filming, I felt sure I was finally approaching a resolution about being in the skin I was in without trying to escape.

We both went off to work on different films in London, and being back home brought with it all the familiar, historical troughs of doubt around legitimacy and identity. I wanted to exist in a bubble with this person that I now loved but it was hard for the bubble to accommodate all the desire and ambition that we had created outside of it. I broke up with him in a panic, then begged him to take me back. I had lost the ability to calibrate what was happening in the present with more reasonable data from the past.

"Love him with loose hands," said my mother, but all I could do was hold on really tight. Then the movie we had made came out and suddenly it wasn't just all the other people who had taken hallucinogens, I was definitely tripping too. I'd first seen the film, alone with Matt in a screening room on a studio lot, a few weeks before its release. Exiting the theater into the Los Angeles tungsten glare was disorienting; the movie had a gravitational pull and I'd felt queasy. All these elements of music and language, story, cinematography, direction, and acting had been sucked into a crucible, and melted into a film that was greater than its parts, yet the parts themselves stayed overwhelmingly brilliant.

Things sped up considerably and I made poor decisions in the jolt of acceleration. I left the kind Irish agent, I left the kind British agent, two women who had only guided me well. I was shedding parts of my life to keep up with the speed, but they were all the wrong parts. I signed up with Matt's male agent.

"That is a TERRIBLE idea," my father told me. "His loyalty is to Matt. What happens when this relationship ends?"

"How can you say that," I spluttered incredulously. "It very well might not end!"

"I just want you to have a plan if it does. I'm concerned about who will take care of you. In the event of your young man *not* loving you, his agent will continue to love *him*."

"That is *so* unfair. It's a professional relationship. He would still take care of me too."

"From what you've said, it's a boys' club. I can see nothing but awkwardness, then another breakup."

"Why are you breaking me up with everyone?"

"Darling, I just don't think you're playing the tape all the way through."

I couldn't slow down, though. My arrival at the "there" I'd always dreamed of—love, working, happiness—was shimmering just up ahead, the grail almost within arm's reach. I just had to keep going at warp speed in case (in my frazzled mind) it all disappeared before I got there.

"What's the end game, Min?" queried Kate one evening.

"To live with this person I love, who is also writing their own ticket creatively, to be free, to be happy, to choose who I want to be."

"Huh," she said, "that sounds suspiciously like a tampon commercial. Remember: they never mention the cramps and the mood swings in those."

"Why is everyone so down on this relationship?"

"Because it's burning very brightly for both of you right now, and that kind of dynamic is pretty unstable. If you're this overwhelmed, he probably is too. We worry about you. You want a lot of things quickly, and speed is unpredictable. I wish you'd slow down. He is not everything and nor is doing every movie you get offered."

I don't know where the idea had come from that everything had to happen now. Sometimes it felt like lightning had struck and that the chances of it happening again were unlikely. I had conflated love with my career, and the survival of both felt dependent on the survival of each.

I careened toward Christmas. We were living in the West Village in New York while Matt made a movie. The heat from constant attention every time we left the house felt suffocating and so far from anything creative. I got into an elevator on the way to see my dentist one day and a woman broke down into heaving sobs when she saw me.

"Oh my God, SKYLAR. Oh my God, *GOOD WILL HUNTING*. That movie, that movie . . . how d'you like them apples, right? RIGHT? It wasn't his fault, but he was meant to love you; you are an angel."

"I'm really not," I said, and her sobs redoubled their intensity.

"How could he have left you . . . HOW?" she screamed. "Tell me he found you in California, TELL ME HE FOUND YOU!" She clutched my arm.

"I don't know," I stammered.

She was in some paroxysm of weeping that really had nothing to do with me, and yet it did. I felt responsible and also scared that she didn't see a person, she saw an effigy. This was the apotheosis of having become someone else. It did not feel good and yet it was the central thesis of so much that I had longed for in my life.

By comparison, the root canal I had twenty minutes later felt awesome.

Pressure building, I left to go and be with my family for Christmas. I returned to the small apartment in New York late on January 2, and by nine o'clock the following morning, Matt had told me he needed space to finish his movie and could I go back to Los Angeles. In the absence of a clear head shot, which would have been painful but definitive, and with no mention of him having met someone else, I didn't hear the breakup in his words. I reframed the entire thing, made myself as small as possible, and forced my way into the sliver of hope I created.

Alexandra welcomed me back to our ancient duplex in LA and put me in the bath. Sitting on the sofa hours later she said,

"He loves you. He just needs space because it's all crazy right now. He'll come back."

"What if he loves me but he doesn't come back?" She was silent for a minute.

"Then you'll get over him."

"How? It's not like I can just go to the other side of town and avoid him. He's everywhere. I don't need his picture by my bed, I got him on a giant billboard right outside my window."

"Yeah. Fuck. Our dads were right," said Alexandra. "Never shit where you eat."

I held on. I held out for the space to be restorative, but all comms with New York had ceased so it was hard to ascertain whether the silence was good in a meditative sense, or bad like a ghost. Eventually I stopped looking for meaning in it, which was then made easier by silence being entirely replaced by noise. Everything externally was now playing out like bad fiction, a love story glamorized and demonized by Hollywood, young lovers thrust into the spotlight, temptation and expectation; a tabloid tale that had had a gaudy cover slapped on it and was now shoved into the window for everyone to see. Our story, which had been a sweet, slim romance, now became a nightmarish blockbuster. I recognized bits of it, but its overblown nature was fundamentally foreign. The story that had been just he and I now became inflated by outside forces, distorted by lack of communication and then, perversely, vacuumed of all reason.

I was now drafting behind the speedy juggernaut of events, heavy lidded and half-awake trying alternately to get my bearings while also trying to ignore the blur of peoples' opinions.

Late at night when no one was around, Alexandra and I would go to the supermarket to do our shopping. One midnight, wandering away from the safety of the cereal aisle, I found myself moving slowly down past all the magazines; shiny covers flanking me on either side, each one bearing the same creepily voyeuristic close-up of Matt locked in an embrace with another actress. The sheer volume of the same image was impressive and I called out for Alexandra to come and see this hilariously over-the-top heartbreak, in stereo, poorly lit and unimpeachably on-brand for Hollywood.

"YIKES," said Alex with a hiss. "They should make a fucking movie about *this*; I'd watch that shit. I mean I'd hate it, but I'd definitely watch it." She cocked her head looking at one of the covers. "Boy, she is really CLEANING his teeth, huh?"

I sat on the phone with my dad.

"It's not NOT working out; it's just not working out how you decided it should," he said.

"How to accommodate the variables, though Dad, am I just supposed to love the Frankenstein's monster version of the life I keep trying to create?"

"Yes. Because it will always look and be different."

"Seems like a pretty straight line for a lot of people I know."

"You don't know anything about it, other than how their lives *look*. Anyone looking at yours would think you're living under a permanent lucky star."

"What about the heartbreak and being publicly dumped?"

"A lot of people would still think that's quite glamorous."

"That's insane."

"Never underestimate the stories people tell themselves about how much better someone else's life is."

"But my heart is broken."

"Yeah. That's agony. Do you want to hear something you won't want to hear?"

"Ugh. DAD. Yes." He always made the hard stuff so tempting.

"The best thing I can tell you is that you're gonna feel this way about someone else."

I stumbled through the next few months, wore glorious gowns to the award dinners where *Good Will Hunting* had been nominated. I made the outside perfect, maybe enviable, occasionally catching my ex-boyfriend's eye across a room in a kind of synchronized loneliness.

However unlikely it had been that love and work and a public breakup would turn out to be anything other than a soap opera, the story did continue to get better and better or worse and worse, depending on how you view soap operas.

I had put our house phone in a drawer where it was now always turned off, and we only turned it on to make outgoing calls. Alexandra's life had become sequestered along with my own, and we drank a lot of wine till very late at night and watched old episodes of *Hill Street Blues*. Consequently, on the morning I was nominated for an Oscar, my sister had to come and batter down the front door and shake me awake with a peculiar mix of joy and irritation.

We stood on the balcony—Alexandra, Kate, our friend Ceridwen, and me—and we jumped up and down. We cheered like football fans, and we screamed like children. The great sweep of LA laid out before us in a hazy crisscross of streets and freeways, pulsing in the heat, forever the passive backdrop to a million moments like this—and all the rest. My neighbor called the cops because he thought we were being murdered, and when they arrived, we all just stood around making bets on who we thought would win the Oscar.

"No offense," said an officer, "but the old lady from *Titanic* is gonna smoke you."

"Yeah, likewise no offense," said his partner, "but it's not gonna be the old lady, it's gonna be Kim Basinger in the Elmore Leonard movie."

"Ugh. Really?" I said. "No chance, huh?"

"Nah, sorry, you were great, and excuse my French, but people got a hard-on for those other two broads."

Shit. Harvey had been right.

Two parallel experiences were then set in motion in the run-up to the Oscars. One was an ongoing celebration with friends, teachers, and my family, a party of huge grins and marveling at good fortune. The other was a waking, cold-sweat nightmare where cameras and microphones were shoved in my face whenever I left my house and I was asked ad nauseam what I thought about my ex and his new girlfriend, how much it hurt, and who was designing my "revenge dress" for the red carpet. I set what I imagined was a smile on my face, and only later, as pictures taken of me screamed back from a newsstand, would I see a kind of stricken grimace staring back. Nervous tension gripped my stomach continuously, I was astonished and disoriented that these two rising tides of happiness and heartbreak could coexist. My brain would try to accommodate with understanding, but when it reached the apex of that impossibility, my stomach would take over and I would throw up in rejection of the whole sorry process.

My parents had come to stay, and they marveled at how I had traversed my life all the way to this moment, and remembered afternoons when I would match Orson Welles word for word as I listened to him reading *The Happy Prince* on a scratchy record. They charted the path they could clearly see now, as if the jumble of my emotional outbursts, a cappella singing, and overly long, postdinner recitals of war poetry could finally be mapped and make sense to them. In some ways they seemed relieved. And while they understood I was heartbroken and sad, the story of their child carving her way to such a moment of professional success was ten times more interesting than a breakup. Their excitement was the thing I watched most closely; it was the only thing that made me feel better.

The day of the Oscars arrived and the steady ritual of preparation made it feel like I was getting ready to be sacrificed. On a tiny break between trying not to cry and thinning my eyebrows to the hard, meager ellipse that was nineties regulation, I stood on the balcony with my mother looking out over LA.

"I'm so fucking angry, Mum."

"You look angry. And sad and beautiful and excited."

"How can it feel punitive? This moment that should be ecstatic, this rare fucking moment is being robbed of all its joy because of a boy."

"Stop swearing, it's so lazy." She took my arm and gave it a squeeze.

"Well, you're not getting out of this. There are two things happening and raging about—the one that is shitty is only going to further hollow out the one that is happy. I think you have to let both things be true."

"It's not fair."

"Aghhhhhh." My mother made a guttural sound of disapproval. Her worldview, ingrained by postwar hardship, extensive travel, and the fundamental, observable inequity she'd seen everywhere, had created an allergic reaction to complaints about life being unfair.

"It is NOT unfair, it is just LIFE," she said, squeezing my arm emphatically on the words "NOT" and "LIFE."

"It is sad and ridiculous, and it is amazing and to be celebrated. That is it. Your expectation that anything is ever untinged by something else is an extremely dodgy narrative to cling to. Let it be messy and painful, let it be joyful and rare. What's the point of life being a multifaceted experience if you keep saying your happiness is contingent on it only ever being one thing—that happiness can only ever have happiness in it. That's just balls—it's impossible, and would be very boring, it would really be just utter, utter *balls*." She put her hand on my cheek and smoothed away some leaking tears.

"For goodness sake," she said loudly but not unkindly, "happy, sad—let it be both."

We went to the Oscars—me, my sister, Mum, Dad, Alexandra, Ceridwen, and Bill. On the way, we stopped at a 7-Eleven for

Cokes and gum and stood in our finery in the downtown strip mall, faces turned toward the hot sun, in slight disbelief that all of this was what we were doing.

Walking onto the red carpet was a full, Roman Colosseum experience. Screaming people in stadium seating, banks of photographers baying for your attention, if not actual blood.

Everybody looked suitably dazed from the flashing of five hundred cameras; publicists and women with headsets herded smiling, unblinking actors toward camera crews and journalists. My dress fell off on some dais I'd been parked on, and in the photo, captured seconds after I grabbed my fake fur around me to cover my boobs, my smile was a rictus of shame and good humor. In the theater, a cameraman set up shop in the aisle by my seat; he looked like he was there for the long haul and had clearly been told to stay on me, as I was sure to be good TV. He wasn't wrong; it would have taken a far better actor to cover up the rampant emotion, and my face through the evening was that of someone watching a car crash happen in slow motion. *Curiouser and curiouser,* I thought as I watched the drama play out onstage, *I'm the drama people are watching at home.*

The category I was nominated in came early on. Dad sat next to me, so handsome in his black tie, so unflustered by the circus. He held my hand, and as the presenter started to read out the names of all the nominees, he leaned over and whispered in my ear.

"Darling."

"Yes."

"You're not going to win."

"I'm not?"

"No."

"Why not?"

"Not your year, angel. Another time, I'll bet. But don't let that camera see you sad, they don't deserve it."

He leaned back in his seat, and we watched Kim Basinger glide up to receive the award. The cameraman at my feet pushed into a close-up of my face, and like a wildlife photographer who has an instinct the animal is about to do something worth filming, audibly held his breath. I couldn't give him the shot he wanted because all I felt was relief. The aperture was closing, the public appraisal and consumption of the drama I'd been caught up in was fading out. There was new meat that wasn't me, standing by, someone else was getting ready for their close-up.

8

HERE, THERE, AND EVERYWHERE

I woke up on New Year's Day with the flu.

I lay in the bath and felt exhausted by another year of chasing some external idea of what I should be doing. The tireless ambition of my twenties had given way to a searing suspicion that there was something else I wanted, but I refused to interrogate it as I was sick of wanting stuff: another role, true love, acceptance, admiration. I lay pruning in the bath, looking out over the deep Somerset countryside, feeling overwhelmingly sad, and longing for the sham of resolutions (particularly having to tell people what mine were) to be outlawed.

Every year, my whole life, I had dutifully intoned my desires for the coming year on New Year's Day—desire being the secular cousin who doesn't wear knickers to church, to resolutions' fire and brimstone—and they had always acted like a placeholder for the nirvana I would reach if I could just fulfill them. The heady, sacred paradise of "there" always dangling ahead of me, like a utopian carrot. All I had to do was scale the whole heap of shit of my own making, plus the wild card of circumstance, and I would arrive.

In the bath, there could have been a eureka moment of clarity, a soulful call to acknowledge the journey instead of fixating on the destination, but I only felt the existential dread I'd woken up with—that coquettish desire and Bible-thumping resolution were gone. I'd banished them in the ticking over from last year to this and finally burned through my long-held idea about success—that if I worked really hard and found ways through and around the obstacles, I'd arrive at the place I most wanted to be. I would know it when I got there. My fever dream then further incinerated all the tributary thoughts around this, until all that was left was the one hot truth, that beyond the horizon there's just more horizon.

There is no THERE there.

My sister found me sobbing in a bathrobe staring out the window at sheep and a group of naked men and women charging toward the lake and a New Year's Day polar dip. They were shrieking their intentions with breasts cartwheeling wildly,

singing their intentions like a song, the attending penises slap-
ping along, completely out of time.

"I think it's really positive. You're not harassing yourself to
reach some goal that you've hung all your happiness on when
there isn't any such goal. You make it all up in your head, Min.
All the fears I've ever heard you be fearful of are things you
made up in your head. Leave your head alone. Just come and
have breakfast and start the year there. Then let's see."

I felt so nauseous and hot I told her I'd just stay in bed till the
Advil kicked in. All I wanted was some direction, I loved taking direction. I wanted to know what I was supposed to want.

Later, lolling in a window seat, retching now and then into a
wastepaper basket, my sister came back into my room and sat
down in a chair next to me.

"Are you throwing up?"
    "Yes."
    "Do you have a temperature?"
    "A small one."
    "Are you massively tired?"

"Yes."

"Do your boobs hurt a lot?"

I clutched them and they felt like giant bruises.

"Yes."

She smiled the way she did when we were children and knew we were both in trouble but whatever infraction we'd been part of had been totally worth it.

"I think you're pregnant."

"No."

"I think you are."

"But I've got a difficult uterus, remember that horrible old doctor compared it to having a U-bend in a toilet and said I'd never get pregnant."

"Fuck that guy. Let's get a pregnancy test."

She hustled me into my coat and gave me a lemon.

"Huff that in the car if you feel sick; totally worked when I was pregnant with Percy."

My sister had two children who were the light of all our lives. She had a husband and a lovely house in Notting Hill. I didn't even have a boyfriend; me and the chap I'd been dating having amicably broken up before Christmas.

"Where are we going?" I asked her as she tore up the driveway of the hotel where we were staying,

"Radstock. It's just up the road. There's a pharmacy."

"But it's New Year's Day. Everything will be shut."

"Sooooo negative, anyone would think you don't want to know if you're pregnant."

"I don't."

Radstock was a ghost town and I didn't think it was just a late night and hangovers that were keeping the people off the streets, no, everyone was home having their own existential Mexican standoff with the expectations of the new year, and them in it.

We parked and walked up the main street, Kate shouting "Here it is!" as we came upon a small pharmacy that was decidedly shut. She peered through the leaded glass windows and caught a glimpse of someone exiting through a door behind the cash register in the back.

"There's someone there!" she bellowed, banging on the glass, then moving to the door, where she weaponized the knocker.

"HELLO, HELLLOOOOO, EMERGENCY!!!"

I felt the familiar horror and delight at seeing my sister in undeterred mode. Honestly, I felt for the pharmacist, and he hadn't even shown up yet. A few minutes of uninterrupted knocking later, and a sash window above the shop opened sharply and a very cross man stuck his head out.

"Oi! IT IS NEW YEAR'S DAY. WE ARE CLOSED. STOP BANGING ON MY DOOR. I HAVE A TERRIBLE HEADACHE AND IT'S A HOLIDAY." My sister moved seamlessly from barbarian at the door to charming sylph.

"Oh, gosh, SORRY! I know, I know, it's New Year's Day and you're closed but honestly, we have a real emergency if you could possibly help us, it would be your first good deed of the new year and would mean so much to our family, I can't even tell you."

She smiled her radiant smile, the smile I'd seen men and women alike be felled by for as long as I could remember. Looking up at the gorgon pharmacist, scowling, nursing his hangover, and pissed off at what was probably an interrupted Bond movie viewing, I thought she might have finally met the unmeltable.

She added a final entreaty that often triggers something in men who feel powerless and underappreciated.

"Please, sir, PLEASE?"

Bull's-eye. He smiled and rolled his eyes.

"Oh, go on then, I must be mad. I'll be right down."

My sister stared evenly at me. She didn't gloat when she got her way, as it was her norm, and nobody had to feel like a loser just because she won. Unless, of course, she wanted them to.

The pharmacist came toward us in his Christmas pajamas, rather endearingly having thrown his white pharmacist's coat over them.

"Come in, come in," he said. "Now, what's this emergency?"

"It's my sister. I think she's pregnant."

"Are you a doctor?"

"No, but I have two children," said Kate, bettering the credentials. "Could we possibly get a couple of pregnancy tests?"

With only mild irritation, as he clearly still wanted to bathe a little longer in the wattage of her smile, the pharmacist said,

"And how is this an emergency?"

"Well, we have to find out NOW to rule out it being any of the number of other diseases my sister has."

"Diseases?" I yelped.

"Conditions," she smoothly countered. "We just want to be sure before we rush her to the emergency room."

"I don't have any diseases," I whispered at her.

"Look, do you or do you not want to know if you're pregnant?"

"I do not."

"She really does, she's just nervous," said Kate, smiling with compassion at the pharmacist.

"Oh," said the pharmacist, "well, I'll just grab them for you."

"Bless you," said Kate.

"Have I seen you on TV?" the pharmacist asked me as we were leaving.

"Um, maybe."

"How does that work when you're pregnant, do they shoot you from the neck up?"

"I don't—" A merciful wave of sickness rose and I had to run from the shop to throw up in the street. *Oh, my God*, I thought, *how will I work if I'm pregnant? How will I take care of a baby, how will I—*. The thoughts were banished by another wave. Soon we were back in the car and heading to the hotel.

"Just do this one thing at a time, Min. Just go and find out."

Even through the profound fear of what this might mean, a keen wonder was also present as I peed on the two sticks. I then sat on the edge of the bath and waved the sticks like Polaroids. My mind was now blank, it was clear, it was unmoving; my whole life, past and present, had come to a gliding halt as one of two potential futures prepared to join the caravan. I looked down at the sticks, and the two sets of parallel lines that told me I wasn't alone in the bathroom. I stood up and looked at my face in the mirror, and I smiled. That was the very first acknowledgment of my baby, an instant human reaction to joy, our first salutation.

It was good we'd had a quiet moment together because it would be the last for a while. I came out of the bathroom and went to find my mother and my sister. They were holed up in a small sitting room off the main lobby of the hotel.

"I ordered tea!" said Kate.

"I ordered vodka!" said Mum. "Which one do you want?"

"I'm pregnant."

Kate shrieked and jumped up in a paroxysm of excitement.

"Oh, dear," said my mother.

My face fell.

"What do you mean, 'Oh, dear'?"

"I mean, Oh, dear, what are you going to do? You're not married."

"But you weren't married to Dad," I said, my voice rising.

"Yes, but we acted like we were and he was there to take care of me when I had you and Kate. Who is going to take care of *you*?"

"I am. I am going to take care of me like I always have."

I was angrier than necessary but desperate to have her tell me this would be okay. Mum was always up for any adventure. She took risks, never wallowed when things didn't work out, and shook off any hardship before getting up and back into life. I needed her to be on this adventure, not telling me I needed a particular version of a man, who, in my story, had never materialized.

"Darling, I'm just worried for you, that's all," she said, coming over and putting an arm around my shoulder.

"Do you know how frightening it is for me to think you're worried about me in this situation?" I cried tightly. "I want you to believe I can do this; I want you to say it will be all right."

I knew she couldn't do it at that moment. The legitimacy she herself had craved was still too deeply entwined in her otherwise egalitarian parsing of the world. She was too proud to admit it—but it came out in surprising moments—that men still felt like the bulwark between her and her own kind of free fall.

I went home to Los Angeles and told my best friend, Alexandra, and my dog, Bubba. They both flipped out in matching states of ecstasy, and I felt a lot better. I had no plan, but this was the plan now. The baby's dad was kind and happy for me, but we had been dating three months and this was not a romantic comedy where two relative strangers accidently make a baby and end up falling in love. I respected that this wasn't in his plan, largely because it hadn't been in mine either (on account of my U-bend uterus) and the fact that there had only been variations on work as an identity these past seventeen years. I walked around muttering the word "mother."

"Mother Hubbard, mother-of-pearl, mother of God, mother-FUCKER."

I went to the doctor to get a second opinion on the sticks.

"Oh, that's definitely a baby," he said, looking at the picture of the ultrasound. "Beautiful."

"What do I do now?" I asked him.

"Well, let's see . . ." He cast around on his desk, which

was enormous, every inch covered in files and papers and pictures of babies with letters of thanks paper-clipped to them.

"Dang it, I thought I had a book that told you how to be pregnant, but oh no, that's right, you already know."

"Cute." My face darkened; "cute" made me want to puke. Literally.

Heading it off at the pass, he said, "You know exactly what to do. Eat well, sleep a lot, keep swimming like you do, come and see me every two weeks."

"Every two weeks?"

"Yes. You're thirty-seven; you are considered a geriatric pregnancy."

This gave me pause. A geriatric, toilet-shaped uterus had made my baby. I was a *National Enquirer* headline.

Waiting by the elevators, I called Mum.

"I'm definitely pregnant and I'm a geriatric like you. So fun to have so much in common, isn't it?"

"When do you know if it's a boy or a girl?"

"Fifteen weeks."

"Oh, God, darling, one piece of advice: don't do the weeks things, so fucking irritating. Fifteen weeks? Just say *four months*! Nobody thinks in weeks, ugh! It's impossible having a conversation with any mother who insists on doing it: 'How old is your baby?' 'Oh, he's ninety-five weeks.' 'You mean he's almost two?' 'Twenty-two months, yes.'"

I laughed and told her I would tell everyone the baby was almost two no matter what age he was. Some bat-eared by-stander must have had *The Daily Mail* on speed dial because the next day it was reported in the press that I was pregnant. Having my personal life regurgitated in the papers for public consumption was an occupational hazard; the only annoying thing about this particular bit of curtain twitching was that I was only two months pregnant, there were seven more to go, and in the alt reality of the news cycle this was going to be very bad, as my news would stay the same for a very long time, and in the celeb/media paradigm this is a punishable offense. I remember reading something as I sat with my swollen feet in a bucket of ice a few weeks before my son was born. The headline blazed furiously:

"ONLY GWEN STEFANI HAS BEEN PREGNANT LONGER THAN MINNIE DRIVER"

I was on a TV show called *The Riches*, which got canceled a few months later. Swirling panic flooded my dreams, and in them I clung to the weathervane on top of 20th Century Fox Studios, which made the show I was on, cursing Rupert Murdoch and watching the chaos rise in the shape of an ocean made of babies and newsprint. I knew that I knew how to swim, but I just couldn't do it. I woke up gasping at the bottom of an abyss. I was alone, which had never mattered to me before, but it mattered now. How could I bring a baby into a place where there was only me defending, providing, and trying to generate income? I needed to ogle married pregnant ladies and see if they had it any safer. Not knowing any, I went to an 11:00 a.m. prenatal yoga class, as that was a known repository for them. It was very peaceful until an actress I vaguely recognized started wailing about being fat.

"Oh, you're not fat, you're pregnant," cooed a few of the other women.

"How am I ever going to get cast in anything when I've got a giant ass *and* a baby?" She was pretty and blond, but her petulant shaming of her body was disfiguring.

"*And* my wedding ring is stuck on my piggy finger 'cause I'm so swollen." All the women murmured their ascent and raised their own hands, in a puffy fingered toast of solidarity. I didn't mind putting on weight; it was shape-shifting, and becoming the legitimate identity of a mother made me suddenly feel more credible as a human. Most of the time, being pregnant, I felt like the figurehead on the prow of a ship, and sometimes like some gentle, bovine creature—large and constantly eating.

The women mentioned their husbands in passing, some of whom wanted to have sex a lot, some of whom didn't, some were apparently "annoying," some were "really supportive." I was the only single woman in the class, and it wasn't exactly shame that I felt, but rather a pushing upstream against the natural order; a sense that I had once again added a degree of difficulty to an experience, but this time the stakes were much higher. What was interesting as the weeks went on was hearing how the reality of the husbands changed as the women did. As our bodies expanded—bigger energy being released into a much smaller volume of area very quickly, like a slow-motion explosion—the husbands became more and more conceptual; a fixed idea, but one that got farther away the larger we got; their true use properly revealed as the grounding weight on the end of a helium balloon's string. I wished I wasn't an outlier balloon. I wished I was tethered to, not a man exactly, but to some force, a shield against the chaos, helping protect my baby. It smarted that my own mother's instinct may have been correct. Maybe, I thought, I just needed a force who had a job that didn't disappear like a mirage every few months. I realized I was that force and for the hundredth time in my life thought about finding another career. This thought dissipated the larger I grew, however, subsumed by the physical job at hand. Filled with hormones and heat, I felt the superpower of creation, and without dismissing sperm as one of its vital components, person-building inside your own body is a one-woman show. I felt invincible, which became the remedy to my fear and saw me pacing around my house late at night looking at my stuff and verbally auctioning everything off for the baby while explaining that we could live off the proceeds for a fairly good amount of time and not worry.

One day at an ultrasound the doctor said:

"So, do you want to know if it's a girl or a boy?"

"No, thanks."

"Okay." He paused and kept ultrasounding, clicking on the computer keyboard, taking measurements.

"Well, she is really big and beautiful," he said, smiling.

"I . . . I didn't want to know the sex," I spluttered.

"Oh, goodness, did I let that slip? Oh, I am *so* sorry."

Apologies were not enough to stop me bursting into tears. I didn't want some guy ripping off the baby from having its first introduction; it wasn't his news to tell. I was upset enough that the doctor wrote in large red letters on my file:

"DO NOT MENTION GENDER"—as if not repeating that I was having a girl would help me unhear the fact. Consequently I couldn't help holding onto the idea that I was having a girl, but it was never mentioned again by anyone. I drifted through my pregnancy alone, and also not alone, a coterie of friends coming in and out of my house with gifts of advice or produce, or some kind of oil for my perineum. I wandered the ghostly aisles of Whole Foods late at night obsessed with finding stone fruit and root beer. My body was huge, I didn't just feel like someone else, I felt like at least three someone else's. It fascinated me. My purpose was no longer work—the hunt for it, then the liquid disappearance into it. My body was in override of all previous iterations and the sheer scale, the unstoppable certainty of what it was doing was powerfully hallucinogenic.

One night, in Whole Foods, needing to quantify my quantity with solid metrics, I weighed my boobs in a hanging vegetable scale. Some guard somewhere, vaguely watching the security monitors, must have gotten an eyeful. I carefully wet-wiped the scale before and after and whistled quietly to myself when one came in at 4.5 pounds, the other at an even 5.

"Impressive," I murmured, "and altogether, the size of a large baby—how fitting."

Two months after I found out I was having a baby, my sister found out that she too was pregnant. It would be her third child, so her matter-of-factness was off the charts.

"Five-pound boobs? Wait till your milk comes in; some-times your balance will be so compromised by their weight you will actually topple over."

She was staying in LA with her two other small children until I gave birth. My mother was also in town and planned to stay with me for the first month after I'd had the baby. I was a little worried about this, as my mother was not really a baby person.

"I'll make the food," she said, "and all the tea."

"But will you help me with the baby?"

"Well, probably not. But I'll do all the other stuff."

"What is the other stuff beyond a new life that we have to keep alive?"

"Oh, you'd be very surprised, they generate so many other considerations, they're like a conglomerate that keeps creating verticals."

"Have you been reading *Forbes*?"

"Yes. Regulation is also a problem."

"Of the baby?"

"Babies, banks . . . we just need some clear boundaries, which is what I was saying: I'll do tea and laundry and baby-generated chaos and you do physical baby stuff."

"How can you not know how to take care of a baby? You had three!"

"I had Sheila." (Sheila had been our nanny.)

"But what about Edward? You didn't have a nanny with him."

"I had Blundles." (Blundles was our black Labrador.)

I gave up, but conceded,

"He was a good babysitter."

I swam in the ocean every day. Weightless, free, my internal furnace cooled; I would float on my back like a shapely landmass and wonder if every single thing in my life was going to happen by accident. I felt like the last thing I'd actually intended was to become an actress, everything subsequently was luck and circumstance; occurrences carved by the agency of something other than me.

Was that why people got married? To actually curate an event they *meant*, an event that was equivalent to them jumping up and down and waving their arms in an effort to get God's, fate's, whoever's attention while yelling "SEE? I AM IN CHARGE OF MY LIFE!," perhaps in the hope that the overlord or -lady would think, *My goodness, maybe they CAN be in charge without us, they certainly know how to throw a party, and LOOK at the piping on that cake.*

There seemed to be arrival points, and you could try to at-tach stasis to them: "NOW I am married. NOW I have a baby. NOW I have a job." *But the truth was,* I thought, *those points were just layovers on the way to something else and all you could do was try to find balance in the constant movement—giant boobs or not.*

I had loosely been calling my daughter "Bel." I liked the brevity of the name and the clear syllable it sounded out. I imagined her small and freckled with a shock of dark hair, wrists with folds of sweet chub, and one blue eye, one brown eye, like my father. I imagined quietly encouraging her to feel safe on whatever ground she stood and teaching her that shifts in terrain had no bearing on how she could choose to feel. She was this tiny, fluid warrior who smiled and cried with her whole heart, then shook it off like an Etch A Sketch and began anew.

I labored for a night and a day and another night, longing to meet her. On the first night, my sister came into my bed-room, which was filled with candles and the stereo sound of soothing monks *om-ing,* and she said,

"Are we having a baby or a fucking séance?"

Mum asked if I fancied spaghetti Bolognese.

My friend Isla, the former child actor (turned rave pro), had now become a doula and midwife. She'd come down from Northern California to help me have a home birth and at this point in the proceedings told me to tune out the sounds and just focus on my breathing.

"Which sounds? The *om-ing* monks?"

"More the spaghetti."

"Okay, okay, but ow, my God, this really hurts."

"All good, all good, you just gotta turn your OW into WOW!"

I sort of wished my sister had been present to hear this.

It turned out my baby was enormous, in general and more pertinently in relation to its exit point, but I still believed the unlikely union between my sturdy Anglo-Saxon heritage and a yogified Hollywood pelvis could deliver this baby into the giant tank of water that stood at the end of my bed. At hour thirty-five, the midwife from my doctor's surgery had shown up, taken my pulse and blood pressure, and announced that the baby was fine, but my heart rate was tired and slow, and it was time to go to the hospital.

"What about the water tank?" I wailed between contractions.

"That's done, darling," said my mother. "This is now."

We arrived at the hospital, and I was given pain relief that can only be described as orgasmic.

"You don't know how bad the pain is until it's gone, huh?" said my doctor, who had just turned up.

"No. SHE KNOWS/I KNOW," said my sister and I in unison.

"Are you ready to push?" he said amicably. It was the second 4:45 a.m. of being in labor—I was so ready.

I had a welcoming playlist I wanted to be playing as the baby was born. The soothing monks were there, and some whale song was mixed in with deep cuts from Johnny "Guitar" Watson and Stan Getz. I told the expectant crowd that I wanted "love" to be the first word the baby heard when she was born, so for forty-five minutes I screeched and panted "LOVE!" in a very active meditation.

"LOVE!" I screamed as the head was born.

"Love, LOVE!" To the shoulders and the arms.

"LOOOOVVVVE!" as the baby fully emerged.

"IT'S A BOY," said my mother. To which I responded,

"WHAT THE FUCK?????"

The baby wailed, clearly having been woken from a nice dream, with a bad word, my very first parenting choice already trashed with an expletive. They laid him on my chest; he was long and very red and had an extremely pointy cranium, like a baby Dan Aykroyd in *Coneheads*. He was alien and astonishing, and I could only stare at him in silence and experience the next thing a mother must learn to accept (after she's said the wrong thing): nobody had told me that the very first thing we do as mothers—the thing we are asked to continue doing again and again in our children's life—is to let go. I was also letting go of my conceptual daughter, the idea/person I had been bonding with for the past five months. Was she there in him? I was suddenly overwhelmed by a strange grief that perhaps I would never know her, and a guilt that this baby here on my chest had arrived into the world a stranger, because I had been busy thinking they were someone else. I wonder why I had become so attached to the gender of my child in the first place? I think it was benignly narcissistic (if such a thing exists). Perhaps, more kindly, it was primal. Being a single mother, thinking I would be raising this baby by myself, the thought of her being a girl—a reflection I had already seen, one I knew and could speak to—felt reassuring; as if, as a neophyte parent, there was at least one thing I understood; as if her gender were my choice anyway.

I looked at my mother, at Isla, and at my friend Tiffany, who had also been part of the strange intense ritual of the past few days.

"He doesn't even have a name. I didn't do any boys' names because he was 'Bel.'" I started to cry, and the nurse came over and said, why didn't I give her the baby so I could have a cup of tea and move out of the delivery room and into a clean bed.

"NO," I said.

"We are not moving anything until this baby has a name. You have to have a name. To start. You have to have a name. Even if they change it later, I've got to give this baby that, right now. Please?" I looked at all my women, all of them completely exhausted but understanding that this had turned out to be the final push.

"Kai."

"Dakota."

"Miles."

"Stone," said the helpful voices.

I looked at them.

"HE IS NOT A CONTESTANT ON *SURVIVOR*."

Then, like a bell ringing out, Tiffany said,

"Henry."

Immediately, as a chiming chorus, everyone said his name,

"Henry, Henry, Henry."

I looked down at the baby, tiny and gigantic at the same time, the culmination of all the love I had ever felt or dreamed of, the person who had suddenly given me tenure for life, and who I knew would bring their own luck.

"Hello, Henry, thank goodness you're here."

9

SEA-BASED INCURSION

All the best things in my life are ocean-adjacent. I managed to find my way in Hollywood because Hollywood is really just a suburb of the Pacific. For every unsteadying moment or teetering high, there has been a retreat into the ocean, where balance has never failed to be restored. I once left Hollywood, ostensibly forever, and moved to Hawaii, where I lived in someone's guesthouse, surfed all day, and wrote music in the evenings. Pursuing work had become the only consistent thing in my life, and when the work became elusive, I had to confront my withdrawal and stop the chase. It was an extraordinary sabbatical that no one in Hollywood noticed, as I had two movies come out that year; I disappeared into the ocean and my shadow stayed in the limelight. When my Hawaiian odyssey ended, and I returned to California with a sandy guitar and leather-soled feet, the only thing I knew for sure was that I had to find a way to live oceanside.

I would get up at 4:30 a.m., make coffee, and then drive

seventy miles from Hollywood to Rincon in Ventura County. There I would surf in the marine layer until the sun burned it off, only making my way back to Malibu when the local surfers at Rincon became too salty toward interlopers like me. In Malibu, I would hang around like a runaway—get a sandwich, more coffee, surf, sit on the beach at Surfrider and talk to the old guys who leaned against the wall there. They'd tell me stories of the late sixties in Malibu, how because the beach and break were shaped differently then, and the ride across the bay to the pier was so long, it was worth facing the wrath of Mickey Dora to try and steal a wave off him.

I was aware that I was hiding and felt a churning self-loathing that I didn't know how to manage the opportunity of success. I knew I felt better when I was in the ocean, though, and would find myself there even on the days when I'd had no intention of going. My dad had often told me to just tread water for a while when an actionable decision wasn't clear. I did this, both literally and figuratively, until I finally got a job that was the down payment for a tiny cottage looking out over a gully and the Pacific.

This place became the anchor I had been drifting without, or the foot of a compass, firmly placed at the center of everything; one I could always stretch out from and return to. Everything else then became tidal, and the vicissitudes of work and love were better understood through that particular lens. I stopped making movies and stayed home to raise my son and get a regular paycheck from network television. I fell in love with an old friend from my childhood and for four years lived quietly and surfed dramatically whenever I could. The specter of the "there" I was always trying to reach began to shimmer into focus. Just as it did, I found myself lying in bed one night with a sleeping boyfriend and the promise of a late October swell the next day; my phone shrilly dinged the peace. What followed was a dump of seven-inch-long texts, sexts, and pictures from the woman my boyfriend was apparently also having a relationship with. I threw the phone at his head, then grabbed it back and raced to the bluff at the end of my street and called my sister.

"God, you pick some weasels, Min."

"He was my friend for so long."

"Well, apparently not."

"Why does it always seem to end up like this . . . some version of this?"

"Do you want the truth or sympathy stuff?"

"Surprise me," I wept.

"It's your expectation of finding a hero mixed with your astonishing power to find the least heroic men on the planet."

"Why the fuck do I want a hero?"

"I dunno, Min. But you've gotta cool it. There's nothing you need to be saved from. It all worked out."

"This is not working out."

"How the fuck do you know that?"

The following day, I went back to work on the sitcom I was in, hollowed out and comedically incapable of being funny. I sat in my trailer at lunchtime and felt around for the emotional shrapnel. Some piece of it was playing on a loop, familiar and unevolved, historic and young at the same time. I tried to get a better view of it and closed my eyes. The loop played this same equation. It was written out again and again, always in slightly different handwriting but always with me as the common denominator.

A week later, my phone rang at another lunchtime and a friend told me to turn on the news. A fire that had started the day before in Simi Valley had roared its way for thirty miles toward the ocean, and Malibu was now on fire. I stared at the drone footage, thousands and thousands of acres burning, brush and homes consumed, then suddenly a live cam showed the motel half a mile from the little community where I lived, on fire, each small cabin disintegrating. I could clearly see that the wind was blowing fiercely in our direction and knew that we were absolutely done for. I sat watching in dumb horror. *Powerlessness*, I thought, that was it—powerlessness over all unruly circumstance; tiny people assuming autonomy over things we could not control; lucky if we could be comforted by the fact that at least we got to choose our response.

I was enraged, I watched the fronded heads of the palm trees explode like fireworks all the way down the Pacific Coast Highway. My home, my neighbors' homes were going to burn to the ground and there was nothing I could do. I stayed up all night glued to the television, texts coming in here and there, information that sounded like it could be true, but was impossible to verify:

"Point Dume is completely gone."

"There's no water in Coral Canyon and they are fighting the fire with dirt."

"The library survived."

"Pepperdine didn't evacuate its students, so most of the water resources are being used there."

No one knew what was true, but from the news it looked like there wasn't much left; that the fire had burned down through the mountains, skipped over the PCH, and could only be stopped by the Pacific itself. There had been a mandatory evacuation of Malibu, and all we could do was watch the news and try to catch sight of landmarks either saved or on fire. For the next two days, the names of the worst-affected streets were starkly printed, uploaded, or read out. House numbers were intoned, and I mentally took myself down the streets of all my friends and started mapping out what was gone. In the midst of all the terrible news, word came in that my corner of the community had somehow survived. Looking at the burn path of the fire, it just didn't seem possible. I called and kept calling as many people as I could get hold of until the story had been corroborated so many times it felt like it might be true: ten men from our community had refused to evacuate and had stayed to fight the fire. One of them had an old fire line and someone else found an ancient, smoothbore nozzle. They flagged down a passing fire truck and asked the firefighters to open the hydrant where the blaze was worst. The fire barreled down on them from the north along the PCH and through the canyons from the east. They fought it for two straight days and nights, using garden hoses where there were no hydrants, wetting down people's rooftops to stop the burning ashes that were constantly blowing in on the thick, smoky air.

Days passed, and nobody could get in or out of where we lived. The roads were closed and scumbag opportunists who had dressed up like firefighters and come in via the ocean to loot houses had forced a no-ship-to-shore order for all and any boats. Even with proof of residence, you'd be arrested if you tried to get in.

My son was safe with a friend, my job was on hiatus, I was ghostlike wandering through the rubble of my torpedoed relationship, looking for missed red flags. I needed to get home. If I could sweep up the ash that I knew must cover my house, if I could see it still stood and stand in its physical salvation, if I could ship in necessities for my stranded neighbors, there was some hope still.

In our community, one FEMA meal a day was being delivered. But people were running out of eyedrops, masks, batteries, fresh fruit. There was no electricity, so they were running out of gasoline for their generators, and also the equally important—chocolate and booze. I started phoning around trying to find a boat and a skipper and was met with a lot of sympathetic but hard nos. Nobody wanted to get arrested, which was fair. I finally got ahold of Lenny, a twenty-six-year-old surfer with a Carolina fishing skiff that served as his business. He too did not want to get arrested, but having been raised in Malibu and somewhat lit up by the idea of an adventure, said he felt inclined to help. He told me he could bring a couple of fishing buddies as cover but that I'd need someone to help me paddleboard our deliveries to shore. He qualified that with a sweetly dramatic "if we make it."

I cast around for whom I could ask. Malibu friends had scattered and were living in various temporary accommodations with their traumatized kids. Town friends seemed unlikely to jump into an icy November Pacific and swim holding a dry bag over their head. I started thinking about people I'd met who were not friends but seemed adventurous and had definitely been arrested before. Feverishly planning one night, I struck gold remembering a man I'd met about a year previously; he was kind of a modern-day Indiana Jones and made documentaries in places of conflict.

We had been at a party and had a conversation about our shared backgrounds—he, having grown up partly in Nassau, me in Barbados. He was incredibly knowledgeable about geography, cartography, and the different tribal cultures he moved through in sub-Saharan Africa and the Middle East, where he had worked a lot. I was impressed that he didn't lecture while speaking about all these places none of us had been to. He didn't patronize the subject matter he spoke about, or his audience either; he struck me as a funny person to have wound up in LA.

"He's definitely a spy," I said to our mutual friend Apple, at whose party we had met.

"Yeah, everyone thinks that," she replied.

I called him up. He was very polite, and we exchanged formal pleasantries like proper grown-ups, even though I burned to cut to the outrageous request I had for him.

"Could you possibly help me with something?"

"Maybe. But I'm not in Los Angeles currently."

"Where are you?"

"Saudi Arabia," he replied. That shut me up. He did not fill the silence.

"Um, cool? That's very far. From here."

"Yeah," he said. I shifted gears thinking a spy would prob-ably appreciate brevity and intel.

"Okay. So I need to get back to my house in Malibu, which has been in the fires, but I can't get in by road and the coast guard has issued a no-ship-to-shore, but I have to get in. I've got supplies I need to get to my neighbors, also, I really want to go home."

"So you're proposing a sea-based incursion?"

"Am I? Yes! I am!"

"And when do you want to do this?"

"Saturday."

"Okay, I'm back Friday. Just tell me where to meet."

"Really?" I stammered. "Won't you be tired and jet-lagged or something?" There was another silence. I wondered if spies got jet lag or were even allowed to admit to it. Then I wondered if his phone was being listened into by a government agency. What if the coast guard was listening??

"I'll be fine, it'll be fun," he said, identifying himself as the perfect person with whom to launch a sea-based incursion.

Saturday arrived and I was nervy from lack of sleep. I had been dousing heartbreak with coffee and long morning runs; now the mantle of balance was beginning to fray. I stared at my face in the mirror and tried to find an appropriate look for a mug shot. I tried for strong and serene and looked absolutely nuts. *Grim-faced scowler it is then*, I decided.

When I got to the marina, Lenny was clearing space and organizing his fishing gear. He helped me unload the two five-gallon containers of gasoline and all the rest of the supplies. We covered them with towels and laid a surfboard on top.

"How you getting this stuff from the boat to the beach?" he asked.

"There are paddleboards waiting there. We'll just load them up and paddle it all in."

"Boy, I hope you have enough time to do all this before they get you."

"Listen, I really appreciate your helping me, but it would be 'get *us*,' unfortunately."

"Yeah, but more you," he replied.

I turned to grab my backpack, which had a towel and some water in it, and saw The Spy walking along the dock. He smiled as he arrived at the boat.

"Hi. I brought a couple of things."

What he had brought were some dry bags, a satellite phone in a bombproof case, and a huge amount of snacks.

"I didn't know how many we'd be," he said. "I didn't think it would be just you and me."

"Yeah, well, no one else was really up for the potential arrest thing," I said a bit ruefully.

"It's fine," he said. "Less people to organize, more peanuts for us."

He took his flip-flops off, jumped down onto the boat, and helped Lenny pack more stuff away. Lenny's fishing buddies appeared and with the boat sitting pretty low in the water now, we were ready to cast off. Chugging slowly out of the marina, a coast guard boat was chugging in for a shift change. The captain spied me and shouted from the bow,

"You better not be going where I think you're going."

I smiled a big, brittle, horrified smile.

"We're going fishing," said Lenny, brandishing a fishing pole. The captain eyed the pole, my frozen face, and the tightly packed hull.

"What's all that?" he said.

"That's bait," said Lenny. The captain stared sideways at him with one bright eye, like a fish.

"Lotta bait."

"Yeah. We brought a lot of snacks too," said The Spy brightly holding up several bags of peanuts and a box of protein bars.

"Okay, well, you have fun," said the captain, extremely seriously. "Stay at sea. You got it?"

"Yes, sir." Lenny stopped just short of saluting and on we went, out of the marina and into open water.

We reached Malibu just under an hour later; it was a clear day, the air soft as silk; a California dream when you looked at the ocean and the sky, a well-lit nightmare when you looked back toward land. The mountains were blackened and smoking, charred brush smoldered all the way down to the highway, and there wasn't a person or a car to be seen. Silence except our boat, and every now and then the imprint of a house became visible; its remnants were set apart from the rest of the black char, the house and all its possessions burned to carbon, the carbon itself then burned to a fine, white ash.

The beautiful day felt haunted or emptied. Not a soul appeared anywhere, the mandatory evacuation having cleared almost every living soul, the silence and stillness eerie, and our boat disturbingly loud. We passed Pepperdine University, its lawns and buildings preserved, a bizarre virulent green island in a sea of surrounding burned black. Its students had sheltered in place instead of evacuating—a college mandate that effectively ensured precedence for its buildings over the empty neighborhood homes. Firefighters will, of course, protect human life over houses. Tiny pockets of brush burned at intervals along the hillside; with no other fuel left to consume, the flames quivered unrelentingly; isolated, enemy holdouts to the last.

We slowed down as we neared the bay where I live. I could see our silent houses clustered up on the bluff above, looking down over the beach. Lenny killed the engine and we bobbed quietly a quarter mile from our destination. We could see the coast guard boat moored in the bay, protecting but also threatening. The Spy, whom I didn't call "Spy" but "Addison," took out his small, presumably government-issue binoculars and stared at the boat in the distance.

"So, there's a mounted gun on the bow, and I imagine someone just said something funny because the crew is laughing." He put the binoculars down. "We'll just wait a bit."

"They can't just hang there all day; they must be on patrol all the way up to Little Dume surely?" I said, with absolutely no knowledge of coast guard patrols. He was back on the binoculars, though, and only said,

"Just wait."

Fifteen minutes later, we heard the engines churn in the distance and the coast guard backed up slowly and started to make a wide turn, heading north up the coast and away from us. Addison looked at Lenny and said,

"I'd give it five minutes, then get us in as fast as you can."

I looked around for the wetsuits I'd forgotten to bring.

"Shit, I'm so sorry, but you're going to have to jump in in your shorts."

The water was cold this November, about fifty degrees, and a strange by-product of my recent heartbreak meant that I liked it. I liked the breath momentarily knocked from me, the imperative of getting it back, the numbness, then the ache, then the burning feeling of rocket fuel in my veins as I swam; my heart proving with every wild pump that it was my strongest ally. Before the fire, without a wetsuit, I'd swim for twenty minutes or so in prehypothermic euphoria. I loved my watery knife edge but did not mean to visit it upon anyone else.

"It's all right," he said. "Give me your T-shirt and I'll put in in my dry bag."

"Are you okay in cold water?" I asked him.

"I absolutely hate cold water," he said in all sincerity and without an ounce of reproach.

"There are paddleboards on the beach," I replied, not having any other prize to offer.

"We'll just swim really fast, grab the boards, get them back to the boat, load the stuff, and then paddle back to the beach."

"Really fast," he said, smiling a little.

"Yeah, REALLY fast," I said.

We hugged the shoreline and started to pick up speed; the only thing that was going to push us out into the coast guard's sight line was the pier abutting the beach where I lived. The pier was a rusty, listing liability, now more than ever, but Lenny maneuvered around it fast, and skidded to a stop in the bay. A sudden urgency overtook everyone, including the two fishing buddies who had been asleep most of the way but now rather hysterically pointed for Addison and me to jump into the ocean.

The water was panicky cold. I was superimpressed that Addison managed to swim while holding the dry bag over his head and really hoped he could breathe. I cut through the water with a speed I'd been saving recently for sprinting away from bad thoughts.

We reached the beach and grabbed the two big paddleboards a neighbor had left us. Addison was stone-faced but uncomplaining, and his demeanor reminded me of so many stoic Englishmen I'd seen grimly exiting the sea in England when I was a child. Those men would have swimming caps and Speedos, some mottled red expanse of skin on either back or belly, and as they stomped past us where we sat on the seawall, they would reply to our "how was it?" with barks of "horrible!" and "necessary!"

The coast guard boat was still visible as we frantically paddled back to the boat, and I knew when they turned in toward the bay next to ours, we would be eminently visible. Lenny and his friends began lowering supplies, but Addison called out,

"Let's do the gasoline first, as it's what they need the most. We might not get more than one run before they see us."

And as if the coast guard's eager ears had heard him from their distance, two sharp blows of a horn shrieked across the water.

We got the containers of gas centered in the middle of the boards, and kneeling behind them, started paddling for shore. I didn't look around to see whether the coast guard were heading our way; I thought it better to not know and just keep paddling.

"Okay, the coast guard's coming our way," said Addison.

"I did not want to know that."

"Why not? Knowledge is power et cetera," he said, paddling furiously.

"It isn't if it makes you freak out. I would rather *not* know, actually."

"Well, maybe if you knew you wouldn't freak out. I'm pretty sure the thought is worse than the actual thing."

"I don't like the thought or the thing, I am just better at

pretending it's all fucking fine!" He laughed in a way I'd always wanted someone to laugh in the face of my shrill fear. It wasn't judgmental or impatient; he laughed with relish.

"Well then, paddle harder, ostrich," he said.

We hit the sand, dragged the gasoline a little way up the beach, and turned to see Lenny and the fishermen waving wildly, and the coast guard making a beeline for us.

"Can we make one more run, do you think?" I asked.

Addison took in the situation for a split second and said, "Yeah. Come on, quick."

We vaulted back onto the paddleboards and made it back to the skiff just as a voice boomed out through the coast guard's loudspeaker,

"STAY WHERE YOU ARE! I REPEAT, STAY WHERE YOU ARE!"

Lenny and the fishermen were hurling bags down onto the boards and froze at the sound. Lenny yelled, "We're gonna have to motor! You coming or going?!"

I looked to Addison and asked, "Are they going to shoot us if we don't comply?"

"I do not believe they are going to shoot us, no," he said.

I'd heard from our mutual friend, Apple, that Addison had been detained in a makeshift prison in the Burmese jungle and had talked his way out with a carton of Gauloises and by recognizing which tribe his captors came from.

"I'm sorry if this gets you in trouble or, you know, shot at," I said to him, but he was already paddling hard back to shore with a pile of bags on the front of his board and simply called out, "I'M ALREADY IN TROUBLE!"

"We'll try to come back for you this evening," said Lenny, who then turned the skiff and jammed out of the bay. The coast guard repeated their order, and for a second I faced the gray boat with its menacing gun mounted on the bow. A man on the deck waved energetically at me. I'd never had the opportunity for much civil disobedience, so, feeling like I must have a credit somewhere, I waved back at him, then turned, held onto the dry bags of eyedrops, whiskey, and chocolate, and paddled away, hard.

We ran fast but heavily up the beach. A neighbor, who'd come to see what the commotion was—ready for it to be true looters—looked exhausted though relieved when he saw it was just me and a cold, wet man carrying a lot of bags.

"Mike! You good?" I asked.

"Yeah. You need a ride up the hill?"

"Yes, please."

"Any booze in the bags?"

"You bet."

"Okay. Well, hurry, 'cause they for sure radioed the police."

In our neighborhood everyone drove golf carts; we threw ourselves into Mike's and he took off up the hill at a sedate clip, which is to say fast, for a golf cart.

"Do you think the police will really come?" I asked.

"I doubt it, but if I see them, I'll tell them it was just you. Coast guard's gonna be mad, though, and they'll wanna get you on the way out. Bet they hang around in the bay the rest of the day."

"Did you see the gun on the boat, Mike?"

"Yeah. Big gun."

"An M2HB," said Addison wistfully.

We dropped all the things we'd brought with us at the community rec hall. It had become something of a command center, with everyone who hadn't evacuated pooling what resources they had. Two guys had already been back down to the beach to get the gasoline.

We then drove through the silent, empty streets—a ghost town of cottages and desertion, with a smoke-diffused sun lighting the whole scene like a zombie apocalypse.

Everything can happen, I said to myself. *Everything can disappear.*

We rounded a corner, and there it was: stoic, small, and blue, awash with ash but standing. Running up the steps to the deck, I thanked Mike quickly as I felt a great lump of tears start to rise in my throat. I quelled them by awkwardly hugging a large hanging basket of geraniums by the door. If Addison thought this was some strange ritual, he said nothing. I found the key, hidden behind my most trusted sentry, an old piece of quartz crystal, and let us both in.

"Wow," he said, standing in the middle of the open plan cottage, "were you robbed?" I looked around at the bare floors and bookshelves. There was no furniture or any lights, just an old teak table out on the deck with a couple of folding chairs.

"My boyfriend and I had just finished redoing the whole place. I waited seventeen years to fix it up and I think the last of the kitchen went in the day before the fire. We were meant to live here together. I think I did it for him, because I would love it however it looks; it's the place, it's special. He wanted something new. NEW—GOOD!! OLD—BAD!!!" I said the last bit wagging my finger like a black-and-white newsreel dictator, except tears had swelled in my eyes again.

"I'm so sorry," said Addison. "Did he die?"

"No, he didn't DIE!" I said with some force. "He's just gone. He was planning a life with me while also planning one with someone else."

"Ah. I just saw the tears and thought he was dead." This made me laugh.

"People cry about breakups," I said.

"Yes," he replied thoughtfully, "I'm afraid I'm a bit of a robot."

"Well, I'm quite dramatic."

"Yes," he said again, smiling, "but it feels like you really mean it."

We swept up the ash. He focused quietly on the job, and even though there was only a giant garden broom to do the sweeping, he cleared each recess and corner with methodical care. I offered him a sandwich, which I'd hastily bought at the last moment. It was a paltry offering for this stranger-helper.

"No, thank you," was his polite response.

"But you must be starving."

"I'm fine, really, I'll just have some peanuts. I don't really like sandwiches," he said mildly.

"Who doesn't like sandwiches?" I said. "Why don't you like them?"

"I don't trust them."

"You don't trust them?'

"Yes. I feel like they're hiding things."

"They *are* hiding things—the stuff that's in them."

"Yes, but there's always something else in there that no one mentioned. In my experience, anyway. I don't like surprises."

"Surprises are a form of aggression," I intoned wearily.

"Who said that?"

"My ex. But he stole it from someone else . . . speaking of untrustworthy."

"Yeah, that guy sounds like a total sandwich."

We sat on the deck in the haze. It was eerily quiet, no birdsong or other distant voices.

"I can feel everyone not here," I said.

"They'll come back," he replied.

We were marooned. The coast guard boat still hung in the bay, clearly forgoing their patrol in the fading light; perhaps waiting to see if we would try to leave. Our swimsuits had dried, and we had T-shirts that had been stuffed in a dry bag, but it was starting to get chilly, and I wondered what would happen.

"I'm sorry we are sort of stuck here," I said.

"It's okay. This is a strange situation, I'm quite enjoying it." He paused, looking out over the eucalyptus trees in the gully in front of my house and then toward the ocean.

"I thought this might have been an insurance scam," he said.

"What?"

"Well, I thought your house had actually burned down, so when we got here and it wasn't, and you didn't seem over-joyed, I thought perhaps that's what it was."

I looked at him incredulously. "That is a terrible thing to think about a person."

He said with a shrug, "People do terrible things."

"They do," I said, and I wished I could have harnessed his even judgment.

I went back inside to look for a bottle of water. Walking through the house, smelling the ruin of so many others in the smoky air, I thought how ironic it was that emptiness had survived.

In a way, it was the perfect vengeance to wreak on a cheating lover; yoked to their deeds and betrayal, they drag those things on into the next version of their life and relationships, hopefully feeling like there's never quite enough room to exist comfortably next to them, always having to manage a pinch of compression. The abandoned is gifted with emptiness. No secrets or remains to awkwardly accommodate, and once the ash is swept, a clear offering to a new beginning.

I had questions, though.

On the deck, now leaning back in our chairs, feet crossed and looking out to sea, I asked him if he minded my asking him a few things about men.

"Go ahead," he said.

"You are trapped here with me, and I am taking advantage of that, you understand?"

"Yes. Willing prisoner. Love a question. Continue."

"Why do men cheat?" He paused for a while before answering, and I realized he was really thinking about it rather than looking for an escape route. Eventually he said,

"Men, in general, have about a thousand bad ideas a day; quite a lot of those are about sex. I can't tell you exactly why, but as a robot, I can tell you it's hardwired into the mainframe. I know all *people* have bad ideas too, but I'm keeping this specific to dudes because I am one, and you asked.

"Each individual has a choice—to act on any one of those bad ideas, or not. So, then you get into why the choice to act on a bad idea is made, and I can really only give you subjective intel about this: either a man is of good character but makes a mistake, or they are of less good character and their bad choices are systemic. I think it would probably help to figure out which one of those you think your ex is."

"Do you think forgiveness has to be applied to both?"

"I think that is entirely up to the person who has been betrayed. But if you're asking me about me, I don't believe in dogma. I think every single thing that happens in our life should be responded to on its own merit."

"I don't want the burden of forgiveness. Does that make me a bad person?" I asked.

"I'm pretty sure it doesn't," he replied.

"Pretty sure, but not definite," I needled slightly. I think at this point a lot of people would have sighed, but he just looked at me with interest.

"Forgiveness is for you. Not them. It's for you to feel better. And if you don't want to feel better yet, to me, that's fucking okay. Definitely."

Some of my knotted assumptions were unscrambling. I wondered if there was further clarity to be gained from this amiable truth machine.

"Do you think men can change?"

"Of course they can," he said very gently. "But I think it might be misguided to base your happiness *on* them changing, particularly if you have seen their lack of change played out for a long time, with no apparent evolution."

Fuck, I thought. *Fuck, fuck, FUCK. Why didn't anyone TELL you this stuff?* I looked at him.

"Why didn't anyone ever TELL me this stuff?"

He furrowed his brow as if it didn't compute. "I'm telling you now."

Then he smiled a huge smile and said, "Let's go and see if the coast guard is still there."

He was tall for a robot oracle and had a determined walk, which I found incredibly heartening, as I myself walk like a Landstrider from the movie *The Dark Crystal.* We stood on the bluff looking down into the bay, and there was the coast guard still, shark gray in the darkening ocean. I was worried now.

"I am so sorry. We are really stuck here now 'cause it's almost dark."

"It's fine. We'll camp."

"There's no water."

"There're two liters under your sink, and we can go for a swim tomorrow."

"Are you always this positive?"

He looked stumped for a second. "No."

"It's almost five," he said. "We'd better go and see if someone can lend us a flashlight and if there's a spare sofa to crash on." I was suddenly hit with a practical, hopeful thought, probably born out of proximity to this robot.

"I think we might be saved," I said.

"By what?"

"Bureaucracy."

A clock somewhere must have struck five, but all we heard was the great rumbling of a boat's engine. The coast guard— subject only to the mandates of the federal government, not their own private vendettas—were clocking off for a shift change.

"I did not expect that," he said, looking quizzically at the boat as it chugged off into the twilight. "That was a pretty binary ending."

"To what?" I said. "A weird potential insurance scam that turned into a bit of a free therapy session for me?" He looked at me and listened to me dismiss, if not denigrate, the day.

"I was thinking that it was an unlikely robot ending to a mysterious adventure," he said finally.

Phone running on the fumes of a battery charge, I texted Lenny. Astonishingly, he hadn't bailed and was around the corner catching the last of the daylight waves.

I locked the door, put my hand on the sentry quartz, and said a silent good-bye to my house.

"Did you just say good-bye to your house?" Addison asked.

"Yes," I answered, slightly defensively. "The house always says good-bye first, though."

We walked back down to the ocean just as Lenny was pulling up in his skiff. Addison put our T-shirts and phones back in the dry bag, and I saw him grimace only slightly at the thought of getting back into the cold, inky ocean. Again, I loved the shock of the cold water, feeling my heart hammer and my legs burn. I liked swimming in the dark with this stranger who knew a lot. We climbed into the boat and stood around with towels, reviewing the adventure with Lenny in the way people do when they've experienced something together and mirror the story back and forth—even though everyone knows the major plot points.

He turned the boat and we sped along the black coastline, no lights from anywhere and no sound but the wind and the thump of the hull on the water. I was freezing, I'd come only in a swimsuit and T-shirt, and the wet towel around my shoulders was a terrible scarf. I was so relieved about the house and my neighbors, and the information about cheating men. The emptiness had a corner that was now filled with something, and I felt the tug of it anchoring me. I must have been visibly vibrating with cold because Addison moved to sit directly in front of me and acted like a Windbreaker. I huddled behind him and thought what a shame it was that I had been finally ruined by heartbreak and would never be in another relationship—even with a handsome, sentient robot. I thought about growing old in my little house and swimming every day like my eighty-seven-year-old neighbor Joyce, and the thought was also a relief.

We docked back in the marina and said good-bye to Lenny and his fishermen friends, then we stood under the sodium-lit streetlamps and looked at each other in the yellowy gloom.

"I'm sorry," I said.

"What are you sorry about?"

"This would be really romantic and everything if I weren't ruined and full of self-pity."

"You don't seem ruined to me; you could probably bring a jacket to your next outing on the high seas, though. Maybe, cast yourself as the victim a bit less." This was harsh but fair.

"I don't want a boyfriend."

"I don't want a girlfriend."

"Okay, good. Can we take the impasse into the back of my car for a minute, then?"

We sat in the backseat. He put his arm around me, and the burn of the water and the fire receded, the motion of the boat steadying to stillness, and the pace of sadness slowing almost to a stop.

We stayed like that for a long time, the day and the night settling around us like ash.

1 0

DAFFODILS

I say, *Daffodils always look like they are shouting.*

You say, *What are they shouting about?*

The end is the end. Spring says something else. I'm confused as to whether this is a way out or a way in; one door closes, another one opens, except the open door is just a clever mural, an optical illusion, a tunnel in a *Road Runner* cartoon that is really a brick wall. I've taken a withering drug and spring is my hallucination.

The windows from my mother's hospital room open into the atrium of the rest of the hospital rather than the rest of the world. I see the eighties architect in his skinny tie, urged on by fast-track construction and late liability clauses drawing in opaque plastic sheeting where the glass roof should have been. The howling wind now makes terrifying kettledrums of them, crashing and banging so loudly and apocalyptically you think you are about to die. The sounds echo through the hospital mall, nowhere to go, shouting at themselves.

This first night alone with my mother she murmurs through the noisy night that never lets up. I lie down, I go to her, I lie down, I go to her. I soothe her because the sounds are so frightening, but I am the only one frightened.

The darkest night: that night we have feared as children. These noises the fulmination of that fear. I feel like if I can bear them, survive them, she will survive. I dig into the plastic tile with my toes, grip metal bed-bars to make her safe, hear my own breath as quick and shallow as hers. There is nothing but us, stranded, still believing in morning.

Saturday

We get a text one afternoon:

Well, my darlings, PLEASE DO NOT FREAK OUT.

It is now in my experience that when you get a text such as this, you should definitely prepare to freak out. It is Saturday, my mother is putting on makeup at her home and notices that the whites of her eyes are yellow, that in fact her whole skin tone has taken on a yellow hue. She calls her sister, which I understand, as my own sister also hierarchically precedes the doctor. Mum's sister, Andra, tells her to call 111, which is the National Health Service information line in the UK. The doctor on the phone advises her to go immediately to the emergency room.

It's such a nice day and she doesn't feel terrible, so my mother decides to ride her bike there. She calls her sister back to tell her, Andra dismisses the bike ride plan with elder sister authority in favor of Mum taking a just-in-case bag and a taxi. A few hours later, after some initial tests and scans, we have reached the all-caps moment of DO NOT FREAK OUT.

We are on our way.

No, you can't come, they won't let you in because of Covid.

But we need to make sure you're all right.

I am in a hospital, there are people seeing if I'm all right every ten minutes. It is extremely annoying.

We'll come anyway, just to be close.

Don't be ridiculous. What will you do, just sit in the car outside? I'm fine, they've only got to keep me in tonight so they can do some more tests in the morning. I'm fine, I've got a bed by the window and the old girl next to me is in much worse shape, poor thing, so no complaints.

Can you eat anything?

No, they said only clear liquids, so I asked for a vodka and tonic.

It's just jaundice, we say to each other, standing in my sister's kitchen. We look it up.

Causes:
Gallstones
Hepatitis
Alcoholic liver disease
Pancreatitis
Sickle-cell disease

Okay, quite unlikely that it's hep A or B, and both are treatable.

Yes, she has never missed a vodka and tonic at 6:00 p.m. on the dot her whole adult life, but she only ever has *one*, so most likely not alcoholic liver disease.

Pancreatitis—might be, but also eminently treatable in the hospital if it's chronic.

Sickle-cell disease—possible but very unlikely; need more info.

Okay, well, it's definitely gallstones says Kate, with elder sister authority.

How d'you know that?

Well, all the cholesterol she eats. Four out of five gallstones are caused by cholesterol buildup and you've seen how she puts half a whole thing of butter on her bread, and we all know she is not scared of cream.

Sunday

Sunday is spent happy with our diagnosis and on the phone with Mum. She says there is a strange upside-down reality on a ward. Patients sleep all day peacefully but then at night they groan and cry out and suffer consciously. Overhead lights are permanently on so nurses can see what needs to be done. The night is exhausting and so, of course, with the advent of the day, tired nurses go home and are relieved by others, the patients finally drift off to sleep, and the whole cycle begins again.

There will be test results by the late afternoon. DON'T FREAK OUT.

Mum's text to us reads:

It looks like there are some abnormal cells around my liver, and a bit of my pancreas is swollen. More tests due.

The Kafka hospital experience makes itself known: *the results of the tests are more tests.*

Okay. Well, that sounds very much like pancreatitis to me, I say to Kate, who nods. I do not go near the abnormal cells around her liver, they are not pertinent to my diagnosis. I am a doctor of only treatable disorders. I shall ignore the cells even though they mean Mum will spend another night in the hospital.

We call Mum. *Will you be able to sleep tonight?*

Kafka #2:

Yes, they actually wake you up to give you a sleeping pill.

We love you, we say, our voices join in unison down the phone, the word "love" emphasized; it is our prognosis, it is our only medicine.

Monday

I am in Waitrose. I have shopped with purpose, my cart is full, I have maintained a safe distance from everyone, including myself. My phone rings. A smiling picture of Mum standing in her kitchen, backlit, hands on hips, and leaning toward me. A young voice says *hello* in the foreground (foresound?). I hear and feel discordance in the back.

I'm a junior doctor.

Junior, JUNIOR, I think. She sounds so young, like she's borrowed her mum's phone, when in actual fact she has borrowed *my* mum's phone.

I'm very sorry, Gaynor wanted me to call you, as she is just taking a minute to . . .

She says more, but I make a sound, and my mother—who must be right there, next to the doctor with the phone on speaker—calls out to me. I find myself felled by all the words. I kneel in front of my shopping cart, and it feels like the next logical step.

Sorry, excuse me, says a man who leans over the top of my head, grabs a can of Bird's custard powder, and determinedly does not look down. The doctor keeps talking.

It's the worst diagnosis and I really am terribly sorry . . .

I look down at the floor and pinch my leg. *Do not cry.* My inside voice is extremely stern, almost shouting at me. Some deal has been struck. *You can stay kneeling on the floor in Waitrose, but you will NOT cry and have your mother hear.*

I speak quite calmly from the floor.

All right, well, thank you for calling me, Doctor. All right, Mama, I'm here, don't you worry, I'm just going to go and get Kate and then we will be right there. We'll sort it out.

I slump a bit farther onto the ground as I hang up. *We'll sort it out,* as if it were some mix-up, some overdraft, some missing piece of paperwork, a larger bill than you'd expected. That's about right, though—late-stage, terminal, dead-end cancer, a much larger bill than you'd expected.

I would so like to stay here on the floor in Waitrose. I keep one hand gripped around the shopping cart's handle, no one looks down at me, they glide easily around me. In England, raw, public expressions of emotion make you invisible. I am a very British superhero. Suddenly I have to find my sister. We have to

251

go and rescue Mum from being alone with this news among strangers, we have to get there and shoulder the news for her; heft it onto our strong backs and give her time to catch her breath.

I pull myself up, the full cart balancing my leaning weight. White knuckles gripping the handlebar, I'm staring into the mountain of shopping. Christ, that is a lot of mature cheddar slices. I push the cart to the front, by the checkouts. I am going to weep. I wheel around. A woman who works for the supermarket stands right by me.

Are you all right? She doesn't see my invisibility.

I don't know what to tell her, so I say a lie that is almost true.

My mother just died.

Oh. She says it low and sad and puts her hand on my arm.

Would you like me to take your shopping cart away? I feel like this woman might be able to fix everything.

Thank you, I say. The weeping starts, and I head for the stairs to the parking lot.

Tuesday

We take it in turns to bring her her favorite things. My mother's outlook is positive.

We've all got to go. They said I've still got some time, though.

They had said this, but in a "How long's a piece of string?" type of way. Astonishing that a doctor could genuinely expect you to get your head around a statement like,

It could be weeks, it could be a year.

How *could* it be that? That is a HUGE spectrum of earthly time, now that we have had our noses jammed up against the fact there is a fucking premium on earthly time. As if before—time here was forever.

Anyway, I say, rolling my eyes and exhaling heavily while puffing out my cheeks. I do this a lot now. I feel like a teenager being passive-aggressive with God.

Tomorrow, Mum will have a biliary stent inserted to relieve her jaundice. It is a straightforward procedure, and without it she will die much sooner, so now, with an entirely new set of requirements for what we deem "positive," we are feeling pretty good.

Wednesday

Nothing-by-mouth on a metal gurney in a hallway. Mum waits all day for the must-have, lifesaving procedure: four hours, six hours, eight hours she waits. It never happens.

Kafka #3:

Me and doctor:

But you said it had to happen today.

It will happen on Friday now.

Friday is the new today?

There's a backlog.

But you said it HAD to happen today.

Now it has to happen on Friday.

Me:

I roll my eyes and exhale heavily . . . *Anyway.*

Thursday

Walk the hallways, Mum leans on me. We stare out across the view of Southwest London.

Try to find my house, she challenges. Mum has always been the keeper and instigator of curiosity, since we were children.

On a boring walk: *Find me a feather, a blue rock, a yellow flower, and a stick shaped like a letter.*

On another boring walk: *Let's just climb this hill and see what's on the other side.*

There was a bull, hunchbacked, staring up at us and too still.

Okay, she said. *NOW RUN!* And we ran, Mum passing my brother, then a baby, to my sister in a fluid football pass, vaulting the gate, catching my brother in another pass, laughing as we scrambled over the fence, clearly delighted with the charging bull.

We turn and walk back to her bed.

Oh, darling, this is no fun, is it? But the daffs'll still be out by the time I am, and then the magnolias. So much to look forward to.

Friday

Kafka #4:

She wakes up from the procedure thinking she is dead.

It is frightening and surprising. It is frightening and surprising when she realizes she isn't dead.

I sit by her bed, holding her hand, and she tells me the story. I remember the times she'd done this for me when I was a child, how she had listened.

Soon, when a hard story has been fully told, it's sadness/pain/horror exorcised, it's ghost ready to rest, it will start to go in circles if you keep on telling it.

Mum's voice gets higher as she grips my hand and relives the same awful details again and again. I do what she would have done, back when I was small and outraged, red-faced with some unfairness or pain, caught in the eddy of my story.

Shhh, shhhh, it's done. It's done. We are here. You are all right. Breathe. I know it was terrible. I am here.

The pieces of parenting she gifted me, without knowing, are pieces of her. Now they are me. Maybe it's not roles being reversed but rather a relay race that goes round like a story, a happier story.

Softly, the light changes outside. Fresh nurses relieve tired ones; the thread of meticulous kindness is picked up. Mum sleeps.

Saturday

My mother is charming. Even in a hospital gown, in considerable pain, worrying about her business, she chats and laughs with the staff, knows all their names, and does all the things they tell her to do. This is a marvel, as she is someone who frequently will leave one of our houses, silently without telling us, should we ask something of her that she doesn't like. Above her head on the white board where stats and the patient's name are written it says "Duchess," with a smiley face.

Sunday

Today she can come home. Home to my sister's, who has the biggest bed. There, we will all get in (carefully) and make our battle plan for this war on cancer we are about to wage.

My nephew Percy and I go to pick up Mum. She sits on the edge of the bed, exhausted from having put on her clothes, elegant and made up, her bag on her lap.

Are we off? She looks desperate to get out of here. I feel what she does: if we can just get out of here, out from under the collected vibrations of the very ill, from the strange, slow pall they cast, we can take a deep breath among the daffodils—the deepest! Clear our heads and once again, quick and alert with life, chart our course.

Bureaucracy, the passive-aggressive jailer of us all, doesn't need to raise its voice when it says,

Not so fast.

The discharge paperwork is wrong. There's another person's signature needed, but they are on a break. The phone at the nurse's station is ringing. You don't exist in our system. We wait for two hours. Mum looks longingly at her bed. She is so tired, and the pall is pressing down upon her, as it is upon all of us.

No, NO, not the bed, focus on the door, the DOOR'S the THING, I say, sitting by her and clearly knowing our fight for her life begins with this primary escape.

Eventually, eventually, paced and played out in slow motion that's also moving through molasses, the paperwork and wheelchair appear. We literally run.

In the car—windows down, the air filled with the nearly blossoming prunus, streets empty because of the virus—we race. The wild feeling of elation that comes with escape. I play the best song ever written. Mum can't believe she's never heard it and Shazams it straight into a playlist for future listening. There is a future again. She smiles, her head resting back, eyes closed, face to the sun. The breeze lifts her hair, the breeze lifts up the vestiges of the hospital, blowing it away. She holds my hand and squeezes it tightly at the traffic lights. We pass many shouting daffodils.

When we get to my sister's house, each moment is deliberate and visible. The things we've done a thousand times—getting out of the car, climbing steps, settling on the sofa—feel rare and new. In the hospital, through all the dismal news and physical discomfort, my mother's appetite remained keen. All she had wanted was roast beef and Yorkshire pudding, something she honestly, hardly ever ate. My sister is making it. It feels like Mum needs some distant memory made real. Maybe it's her childhood; infrequent, delicious food always having been the light-filled moments between rationing and the war. Beef being the pinnacle of treats.

Will you make the gravy? Kate asks.

Sure, I say. I haven't made it in twenty years, but my hands do the work deftly, with their own knowledge. Stirring the sauce, I hear my mother's voice upstairs, her grandchildren moving around her like kittens. I remember her saying: *It's all a decision. You just decide, and then you do something. You don't have to know everything, but you do have to begin.* Make gravy you don't remember, live while you're dying, fight the unassailable.

When dinner is ready, Mum descends the stairs supported and coached down each slow step by our kids. We sit together and the table is golden. The most perfect food conjured from memory. We toast her escape, our escape. We celebrate this moment, nothing is bittersweet: no thought for the shortened future we have with Mum, time is only here in this moment and it seems to me we are all so sharply alive.

Mum smiles and eats, I can see how profoundly tired she is, but her hunger triumphs. Never one to waste food, she did, however, always leave something on her plate, for the sake of appearances. But tonight she eats everything. It's strange, she is unabashed, and after a week of being poked and prodded and operated upon it feels magical that she can eat this heartily.

All we have wanted is to have her home, home, which is no synonym for sickness. Home, where safety and strength and protection rule. Our army is the comfort of the familiar, and this is how we will help fight the approaching battle.

We all the climb the stairs to bed. Our kids have turned my sister's bedroom into a candle-lit sanctuary. They show Mum around like tiny hotel managers. They tuck her in, gently and parentally. She is childlike in my sister's giant bed. Soft white everywhere, her eyes closing. We leave the room, murmuring love. I walk back downstairs knowing something is happening: In all the chaos of facing death and the smell of hospitals, real time paused. The past was frozen, the future still inanimate, we had entered into a time of our own creation, and I am only just realizing it. I wonder what is sustaining it, I wonder how long it can last.

Monday

Real time unpaused. There was a split second between the peace and the pain beginning again (this time terrible and in earnest), and in it I watched us exit from our time out of time and then faintly, in the back of the ambulance, I saw the gift that it was: a magical last supper that we celebrated as though it were the first, a fairy tale where the dying were well for as long as the spell lasted, hope and joy replaced fear and sadness, and food that had been impossible to eat was savored to the last bite.

Tuesday

All day, rushing through the cavernous mall of the hospital either to get in or get out. Are we letting go or fighting? Which is it? What tools are needed? Is it breath and compassion or an axe of resolve? No one tells us. We flounder, bedside, and heave quietly in the airless bathroom.

Wednesday

There is a place in the ward called "the family room," where you go to do whatever it is you must not do around all the other patients and your mum. There are no windows. There are large boxes of tissues. It is a hard room to sit in, but on the opposite side of the corridor there is a room that is worse.

We have seen people come out of there: slack shouldered, grim-eyed, and weeping, followed by milky-faced young doctors who are still learning how best to deliver their blows.

They come to find us early in the day and ask to speak. We head for the family room, and as we go to turn left into it, the doctors turn right and open the door into the room opposite. The room is big and light, and in contrast to the rest of the ward, which is beige-washed and halogen-lit, it has virulent lime-green seating and primary-colored blinds. Colors that are clearly there to defibrillate you when the news stops your heart.

They do everything right. They lean forward, their voices tuned to compassion, they tell us everything clearly and steadfastly. Mum has developed an infection from Friday's procedure, from which she will not recover.

Kafka wins:

The thing implanted to save your life, kills you unintentionally.

When they say how sorry they are, I believe them. We cry.

But I am really thinking:

WHAT ARE YOU SAYING AND WHY ARE YOU SAYING IT IN THIS ROOM THAT IS AN ASSAULT? AND WHY ARE WE CRYING WHEN WE SHOULD BE ROARING? WE SHOULD BE ROARING: WHO IS DEFENDING THIS LIFE IF WE ARE CRYING?

Something happens between the time we leave that room and arrive at the single side room where Mum has been moved to. It is a realization as calm and clear as the sea by which I live: there is no "why" now, no space for that word and all its begging. We are now in a corridor and must just walk together. All the grief needs to be put in escrow, claimed later; now we are companions.

We all move into the room with Mum. Flowers, food, chairs dragged in from other places, coats, bags, limbs, draped and strewn. We bring our life, her life, into this place. We watch soccer, and her beloved Liverpool beat Leipzig 2-0, breaking a five-game losing streak. She flashes huge smiles at my brother with each goal and they are in soccer paradise. I step outside to find a wall to lean on and ask my brother-in-law how long he thinks it will take. He leans with me and quotes Liverpool's manager, Jürgen Klopp:

We're going to play till the final whistle.

It's nighttime and everyone leaves, but I stay. A nurse and I drag a thin plastic mat onto the floor by Mum, and an orderly gives me some sheets and a pillow. The wind, which has howled all day, begins to really roar. I lie there, on guard, frightened but ready for a fight—with what? Death? The wind? I'm furious with the hospital's architect and the gentrified tarpaulin they thought fit to serve as a roof. They are who I would like to fight. I barely hear my mother call out, but when I do, I am up in one fluid shot, a movement that's quick and superhuman—the way I moved when I heard my newborn son cry in the night.

Yes, my mama, tell me?

Min, my lovely Min, I'm dying, and I want my breakfast. I'm sitting in a chair next to her with my head resting on her shoulder and I tell her quietly,

Well, I can do something about one of those things.

Can I pick which one? she says, holding my hand tightly.

Yes.

Make the bacon nice and crispy.

We make a menu from all the places we have best loved the food.

Pizza in Naples.

Sunday lunch at Kate's.

Steak au poivre at La Coupole.

Toast from anywhere.

All night as she weaves in and out of sleep and deep pain, we talk about food. The nursery food of her childhood, learning to love the disgusting when everything good was rationed during the war, a lifelong love of butter and how bread is good, but really just a butter vessel.

Do you remember getting fish and chips in the rain in West Wittering? she says.

Yes, you made us take off our sweaters so you could stuff them up underneath your coat and pretend to be pregnant and go to the front of the line.

Well, it was raining, and the line was very long. I did drop all the fish and chips on the pavement and your cardigans fell out and everybody looked like absolute thunder . . . instant karma. She drifts, *Oh, I loved John Lennon.*

We stay, encircled by each other's arms, a closed loop of comfort.

No one tells you how birth and death are so closely aligned. Here, lying in the dark, I see it: pain, a journey that goes toward only one thing and the deep need to have someone with you to hold on to. Humans fret about and question what happens beyond the "end"—never about what came before our beginning. Closed loops. Infinite human experience of beginning and ending, so deeply connected, only one instilling fear.

I am not frightened anymore. We are on an adventure, and this is not some eleventh-hour reach to spin death into a more palatable destination. We are together, this person who was my portal into life. This rare, funny, independent creature who would do the same for me: walk with me as far as she could and then wave me off with love, safe in the knowledge that life had equipped me with everything I needed to meet death as the newest of my many experiences.

Gray light filters down through the opaque tarpaulin roof, into the atrium and through the window into the room where we

lie. We unclutch slightly, now that we are here in the morning. I find a playlist on her computer, music from the forties,
Billie Holiday—"Lover Man" and "Strange Fruit."

Oh, dear, she says.

What?

No, just 'Oh, dear.'

We listen to the music and I balance on my side on the edge of
the bed, careful of all the lines going in and out.

I'm sorry, darling.

What are you sorry about?

Being a shit mother.

This is something she has said and worried about my
whole adult life. Sometimes she makes herself a victim of the
thought and sometimes it carries a deep plea for forgiveness. I
had always been exasperated by the statement and felt it asked
me to repeatedly qualify that there had been shit moments of
selfishness that accompany any human, mother or not, but that
she, in all honesty, was not a shit mother.

There are clearly certain thoughts that keep playing through a life, though, like songs on repeat. They are for you, and you alone and however much you try to involve other people in them, they really have nothing to do with anyone but yourself.

Here, in whatever end-of-life moment we are in, it is suddenly necessary to lay those thoughts to rest. Take the stylus off the record, delete the playlist.

There's nothing to be sorry about, Mum. So what if you were, what if it were true? Does it matter? Because here we are together, talking . . . together. I love you and more than that, I know I love you, and I see who we are together—we laugh a lot, you are who I want to call when things are bad or good or interesting. So how can you being a shit mother really be something that carries any weight in terms of what it did to me, your child?—It didn't. Which makes me think you weren't, or at least, not entirely.

She has fallen asleep, but she is smiling. I think even though it was a bit of a ramble, I made a good point. In making it, I realize I absolutely mean it.

Thursday

My whole family fills Mum's room. We sit around watching her, like she's a TV. My aunt Andra says: *I've always thought when I'm on my deathbed it'll be so annoying to have people who aren't about to die sitting around staring at me.*

Mum laughs. *Turn the bloody TV off,* she says.

No, says my sister, kissing Mum's hand. *Keep the TV on.*

We decide to have a party.

I would like vodka and tonic and cucumber sandwiches, Mum announces. A discussion begins between her and two of her sisters, about how their mother used to make cucumber sandwiches.

Peel the cucumber.

No, DON'T peel the cucumber.

Slice them thinly and then soak them in vinegar and sugar.

White bread, very soft, salty butter.

We go to the shops. Exiting through the doors of the hospital feels like stepping from inside into another inside. There is no stepping outside this experience, I feel quite clearly that I am still in the room with Mum, even as I stand in the rain. We are hermetically sealed into this other reality; we don't leave it until it's really time to go. Until the door appears. I think about the Helen Keller quote we only ever say part of, *When one door closes, another one opens*. That's what we all say; the actual quote is: *When one door of happiness closes another one opens but we often look so long at the closed door that we do not see the one that has been opened for us.* I walk down the street in my bubble; amazing to be in two places at once. When the door opens I think, *I will try to keep looking at it.*

That night, after all the vodka and morphine, as Mum slips into and out of consciousness, I lie next to her trying to help as she rides the waves of pain that come like contractions.

I've had such a butterfly life, Min, beautiful, transient.

Suddenly I am shocked at the sound of her using the past tense to describe her life. Are we already in this place where life is past and the future is right there, but has nothing in it that we have known? I do not want to let her go. I feel this as clearly and viscerally as I have ever felt anything. I think again of that thing no one tells you about birth—that as your body offers up your child to the outside world, your very first job as a mother is to let go. I really never thought about the fact that that gift, if you're lucky, needs to be returned in kind.

Friday

Friends visit. Unspoken goodbyes that take the form of stories from the past and laughing. Laughter vanquishes sadness.

Saturday

It is nighttime. My sister and I drag the plastic mats into the room. We lie down in our clothes and take it in turns to get up when Mum stirs.

Do you remember when she did that 23andMe DNA test, Min?

Yes, I made her do it so I could check we were actually related. She said, 'It's only going to confirm that I am fifty percent red lipstick.'

We laugh in the dim light.

I am so glad my sister is here. There has been a shift, Mum is getting farther away, and it's more bearable to have another witness—you might not believe it if you were only by yourself.

At 2:00 a.m. Mum wakes up and says, *I'd like my breakfast.*

What would you like? asks Kate.

Scrambled eggs, says Mum with gusto before falling back asleep.

The nurse who is in the room adjusting a monitor says very quickly, *I don't think that's a good idea, she is not swallowing well, and she might choke.*

I think she can manage, says Kate. *She had Jell-O an hour or two ago, they can make the eggs very soft, and I mean, what's the worst that can happen?*

Nobody would have enjoyed this justification more than our mother. Gallows humor, on the gallows, would have made her laugh.

How are you going to get scrambled eggs in the middle of the night? I ask, although I don't really need to, as my sister will always find a way. In fact, the more difficult the task the more easily she finds a solution. It has always been this way—as if impossibility were the actual fuel she uses to fix things.

She finds an all-night café around the corner from the hospital and calls them up. The woman is sweet, she will make the eggs soft, and then she'll walk them around to the hospital. Kate hangs up the phone.

Well, this is good, isn't it? We're doing something, she says.

We are doers. Mum: the nascent point of that ability. She is why we can stand here in the middle of her last night and do anything at all.

Kate goes down to the lobby to get the middle-of-the-night breakfast. Mum whispers something and I lean into her.

She holds my hand lightly. We have the same hands, nimble with short nailbeds, they have always looked old before their time because of our freckles, they are very good at making things. She squeezes my/our hand.

Everybody wants it to be more than it just being a journey, Min. But that's what it is.

Death?

Life, she murmurs.

That's the meaning of life, it's a journey?

Yes, beloved. Just need strong feet.

I have pretty strong feet from surfing, I say, but whatever I then babble on about, taking the line of practical and physical understanding of what she said, not yet able to feel the grace of her simple direction, is just sound, as she has fallen back deeply, deeply asleep.

Soft scrambled eggs in the middle of the night. We feed her and stand by like sentries in this backward nursery. Except it's not backwards, it's forward-moving, it always was. It's only now, though, that I see the relay race we were running is up to speed. That at some point, which sprinted by unheralded, she passed on to us—in a fluid motion that must have taken her over her own particular finish line—the role of protector and caregiver, the role of vibrant, vital woman.

I feel so young, here with my sister and mother. I don't remember the last time we were alone together, but it is so familiar. I feel the old fractures: their more slender, older, blonder complicity. My lumpen, frizzy-haired conspiracy theories of exclusion that were sometimes true. My voice loud in the backseat; them turning the radio up and singing a song I didn't know. I feel the laughter too. We are funny people; we can make other people laugh; but no one knows the jokes about ourselves, about each other, as quickly or as deeply as we do, no one understands why they are funny. The night gets darker still, Mum's pain grips all of us. We start to sing, me and my sister; all the songs we sang as kids. Songs from the car, from our bedroom and the bath, from recitals and from cultures not our own whose music was the best thing we took home from holidays. We sing a song I wrote called "Beloved"—a song written for no one that now belongs to her. Swaying and singing: my dear, kind, capable sister and I keep the darkness at bay. I sing and secretly pray for morning. *I can't fight the night anymore,* I think, then *Myself* rears up and calmly, strongly, with a hand on my shoulder, asks me to pull myself together and sing something she'd like. I sing "As" by Stevie Wonder and whisper my I love yous between verses.

Until the day that is the day that are no more
(Loving you)

Until dear Mother Nature says her work is through
(Loving you)

Until the day that you are me and I am you
(Now, ain't that Loving you?)

By the time I get to the "Always" callback, I see that it has only taken the very weakest light of dawn to completely vanquish the dark. *The solution to a problem is never commensurate with the size of the problem.* She told me that while I was facing some impossible thing that was (of course) ultimately possible, because here I am. Here I am loving her, thanking her for everything, being glad that she never minded repeating the solution to a lesson I couldn't seem to learn, never minded my determination to get her to agree with my failure, swatted it away with love and told me with her giant smile that I was terrible and perfect like everybody else.

> *Until we dream of life and life becomes a dream*
> *(Always)*
>
> *Until the day is night and night becomes the day*
> *(Always)*
> . . .
> *Until the day that is the day that are no more*
> *(Always)*

I will not say good-bye. Always.

Sunday

ACKNOWLEDGMENTS

I would like to thank Addison O'Dea and Henry Driver, who shared a house with me throughout the sometimes grim-faced, always slightly hysterical, late-night pacing endeavor that was me, writing this book. Their kindness, enthusiasm, and help are the only way I managed to finish it, particularly after my mother died in the middle of the process. I love you both with my whole heart and will always be grateful that you told me to "make the letters bigger" when I was running out of time.

My sister Kate, who is not only the great North Star of this book, but the best sounding board I could ever have wished for, deserves thanks beyond the words I've got. She and our mum were the first people to read the first pages, and their laughter will always remain the greatest barometer by which I measure success.

Thanks to my friends Emma Forrest and Robin Beth Shaer, whose objectivity and practical brilliance as writers gave me gifts that show up all over the book.

Immense thanks to my agent, Cait Hoyt, whose guidance and patience go well beyond agenting. And to Shannon Welch, who believed in the original shape of my work and then helped me make it recognizable to everyone else. I am also very grateful to Sydney Rogers for stepping in so calmly when plans changed, for being a constant ear and brilliant font of ideas.

To all these people above, who only ever worked to make this book better and had all the patience when I did not. Thank you, squared.

And lastly, to my great friend and manager, Jason Weinberg, who called me up on day four of the lockdown in March 2020 and said: "Ok, what else you got?" and then told me with the certain joy of a very jolly soothsayer that I should write this book. I love you.

Thanks also, to every teacher I ever had.